easy indian cooking

101 FRESH & FEISTY INDIAN RECIPES

Hari Nayak

Photography by Jack Turkel

TUTTLE Publishing

Tokyo | Rutland, Vermont | Singapore

contents

introduction

Traditional Indian cuisine has its own charm, its own signature dishes and its own stories. When we add the twist of contemporary presentation, a touch of native sensibilities and a dash of the global bounty, what you find before you is a kaleidoscope of delectable, modern, yet soul-stirring cuisine, I affectionately call this "easy Indian cooking."

This book represents my take on modern Indian cuisine, marrying together the traditional Indian soul with the contemporary lifestyle. Whether cooked for family or guests, the recipes in this book alleviate that feeling of intimidation that is often associated with Indian cooking.

Easy Indian Cooking re-creates classic Indian dishes using simple techniques along with a delicious juxtaposition of non-Indian ingredients. I have strived to bring traditional cuisine to accessible levels fit for modern living and entertaining, while keeping the flavors and authenticity intact.

Having traveled extensively within India, I'm able to offer you various distinctive styles that are unique to—and often characteristic of—different regions of the country. I've been mindful of the different ways we approach food, how we cook and eat, and the ingredients that are readily available at your local grocery. What results is a contemporary style of cooking great tasting food for easy entertaining and busy lifestyles. Through these recipes you'll experience the richly diverse, culturally beautiful country of India and the many flavors that it can bring to your table using locally available ingredients.

indian cooking techniques

The heart and soul of Indian cooking is the mastery of using unique and imaginative spices, seasonings and flavorings, and learning the nitty-gritty of Indian cooking techniques. You will already be familiar with many of these cooking techniques from your own everyday cooking. The main techniques are steaming (*dum*), tempering (*tarhka*), roasting (*bhunnana*), frying (*talna*) and sautéing (*bhunao*). Other common techniques are the roasting and grinding of spices, browning onions, garlic and meats, and handling sauces. Some or all of these methods may be necessary to prepare an Indian dish. They are not hard to master, but is important to understand the basic principles of each.

Browning

Most Indian recipes require the browning of onions fried over medium-high heat. Evenly browned onions are more flavorful and give sauces a desired rich, deep reddish-brown color. The same goes for garlic—the flavor of garlic is quite amazing if it is fried in oil until it turns golden brown. For the best flavor and color, meat is also browned. Browning also sears the meat, which makes it juicy. I like to brown marinated meat before combining it with other ingredients. If I am cooking a larger quantity, I brown a few pieces of meat at a time in hot oil and set them aside. I then add the browned meat and all the cooking juices back into the pan with the other ingredients and let it finish cooking in the sauce.

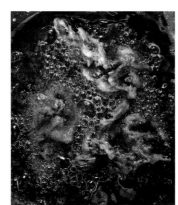

Deep-Frying

Talna refers to deep-frying, Indian style. Generally, for deep-frying, Indian cooks use a *kadhai*—a deep pan with a rounded bottom similar to a wok. Unlike a deep fat fryer, the size and shape of the *kadhai* does not allow large quantities of food to be fried at one time, which results in even frying.

When deep-frying, oil should be heated to between 325° and 350°F (160° and 180°C). This is crucial—if the oil is too hot, the outside of the food will brown very quickly, leaving the inside uncooked; and, if the oil is not hot enough the foods will absorb oil and become greasy. When frying, do not overcrowd the pan; fry the food in batches, if necessary. Use a slotted spatula or spoon when removing fried food from the oil, and hold each piece against the edge of the pan for a few seconds. This allows excess oil to drain back into the pan. Place fried foods on a tray lined with paper towels to drain. To re-use the

oil, let it cool completely. Using a fine-mesh strainer, strain the oil into an airtight container. Store the oil at room temperature.

Roasting Meats

In Indian cooking roasting is traditionally done in a charcoal-fired *tandoor* (clay oven), which gives a unique flavor to roasted meats, breads and vegetables. The juices of the meats drip and sizzle on the charcoal and the smoke that is created gives the food its unique flavor. For home cooking, an open charcoal grill is good substitute for cooking meat kebabs, vegetables and paneer, though the flavor is milder than that achieved in a *tandoor*. An oven can be used to make breads and also to roast marinated meats and vegetables.

Steaming

Dum cooking has been described as the "maturing of a dish," as in this technique the food is very slowly cooked in its own steam. Traditionally, the lid was sealed to the cooking vessel with a flour-and-water paste to make sure moisture stayed trapped within. The vessel was partially buried in hot coals and, to ensure the food was evenly surrounded by heat, some hot coals were placed on top of the lid. Today the modern oven is used to perform the function of providing even heat. The dish is first cooked on a stove top and then well sealed and placed in the oven to continue cooking in its own steam. The advantage of *dum* cooking is that because the vapors cannot escape, the food retains all of its delicate flavor and aroma.

Roasting and Grinding Your Spices at Home

Roasting (or toasting) is the key to enhancing the flavor of spices. It removes the raw smell that untreated spices tend to have and intensifies their flavors by heating up essential oils. All you need is a small, heavy-bottomed skillet (cast iron works great). No oil is used when roasting spices. Whole spices are put in a dry skillet and roasted over medium heat until the spices turn a shade or two darker and become

aromatic. The spices are then immediately removed from the hot skillet to avoid over-roasting them.

In my kitchen I generally buy the spices whole and then grind them myself as I need them. Because

spices retain their flavor and aroma much longer in their whole state rather than when ground, grinding roasted spices in small batches is the ideal way to use them, and gives the greatest possible flavor to

dishes. Traditionally, spice grinding was done with heavy grinding-stones or a mortar and pestle. To save time, I grind spices using a spice grinder, though a coffee grinder works equally well.

Sautéing

Unlike classic French sautéing, *bhunao* is a combination of sautéing, stir-frying and light stewing. It is the process of cooking over medium to high heat, adding small quantities of liquid, such as water or tomato purée, and stirring constantly to prevent the ingredients from sticking. Almost every Indian recipe needs *bhunao* at some stage, and some at more than one stage. Generally ingredients like onions, ginger, garlic, tomatoes and spices require *bhunao* to extract the flavor of each of the ingredients in combination with spices and to ensure that the *masala* is fully cooked before adding the main ingredient. Sometimes the main ingredient, such as poultry, meats or vegetables, may also require *bhunao*. The process of making *masala* is complete only when the fat leaves the *masala*, which is critical in Indian cooking. Traditionally a *kadhai* (Indian wok) is used for this technique, but a heavy-bottomed saucepan or other deep-sided pan, such as a braiser or Dutch oven, works as well.

Roasting Vegetables

Use fresh and firm vegetables (peppers are a popular choice). Take a sharp knife and remove any stems, cores, membranes and seeds. Cut items like peppers in half lengthwise and flatten the halves by squashing them against a flat surface. Lay the items skin-side-up on a foil-lined baking sheet and broil, 4 to 6 inches away from the heat source, until blackened all over, 5 to 10 minutes. Watch carefully and rotate the pan as needed to blacken as evenly as possible. Pull up the edges of the foil to make an envelope around the vegetables. Seal the envelope, and let it sit at least 15 minutes and up to 1 hour to soften the items. Pull off and discard the skins. Do this under running water, if you prefer.

Tempering

This technique is unique to Indian cooking. A mixture of whole spices, with or without chopped garlic and ginger, is added to very hot oil. This extracts and retains the essence, aroma and flavor of spices and herbs. This process is performed either at the beginning of cooking a dish or after the preparation is nearly complete. If done after a dish is cooked, the prepared tempering is poured, sizzling hot, over the dish to add a burst of flavor (as is sometimes done when preparing *dals*). The seasonings that are most commonly tempered include cumin seeds, black mustard seeds, fennel seeds, dried red chilies, cloves, cinnamon, cardamom and bay leaves, as well as chopped ginger, garlic and fresh or dried curry leaves. The ingredients are usually added in rapid succession, rarely together. This is to ensure that each ingredient is fully cooked, and thus its flavor fully extracted into the oil, before the next ingredient is added. This method also allows for longer-cooking ingredients or spices to be added first, and shorter-cooking ingredients or spices—which would otherwise have the tendency to burn—to be added last. The crackling of the spices or a change in their color indicates that the process is complete, unless fresh herbs and vegetables are also being used.

You don't need special kitchen tools or cookware to cook Indian food at home. All you need is a well-equipped kitchen with sturdy skillets, pots and pans with lids, tongs, good knives, graters, mixing bowls, a rolling pin, a perforated spoon, a sieve, a strainer and a citrus squeezer. I like to use an Indian spice box to hold my most frequently used spices and spice blends—garam masala, cumin seeds, mustard seeds, Asian chili powder or cayenne pepper and turmeric. It sits on my kitchen counter where I can quickly grab a pinch of spice when needed. I generally use non-stick pots, saucepans and skillets when cooking Indian food at home because of the relatively long cooking time of ingredients. Some ingredients, like spices, onions, ginger, garlic and tomatoes, which are typically cooked in small quantities of liquid or fat, tend to stick to conventional pans. If you have regular pots and pans, to prevent sticking, make sure they are heavy bottomed and sturdy. Stir the food frequently, and add more cooking oil as needed.

The following additional tools are not crucial but they will make cooking Indian food a lot simpler and quicker.

some helpful tools

Blender

When it comes to combining liquids with fresh herbs or spices for sauces, pastes or purées there is nothing more effective than a blender. Blenders with a narrow, tapered base (or basically straight sides) work very effectively to purée thick sauces and pastes, unlike the blender jars with a broader base, which are ideal for blended drinks. Ginger garlic paste can be made very efficiently in a blender. I also use it to grind large amounts of whole spices. I prefer glass blender jars in my kitchen as plastic absorbs aromas from the spices and herbs.

I also have a hand-held blender, also called an "immersion" blender, which I often use to purée vegetables, lentils or beans. This tool is ideal when preparing puréed soups or *dals*, as you can purée the food directly in the pan. You need not wait for hot liquid to cool to use an immersion blender, and it saves you the task of cleaning up a messy upright blender.

Electric Food Processor

The traditional heavy grinding stone of Indian kitchens, which is moved manually, is now replaced with the modern food processor—a time-saving tool par excellence for busy cooks. Essential ingredients like onion, chili peppers, garlic and ginger can be made into pastes very quickly in these machines. The food processor can be used to chop or mince vegetables and fresh herbs, cutting down considerably on prep time. I recommend a food processor that has a capacity of between 7 and 10 cups. To pulverize smaller quantities of ingredients, make sure the blades sit close to the bottom. For very small quantities, use a knife.

Electric Spice Grinder or Coffee Grinder

I highly recommend investing in a spice grinder or a coffee grinder. This is one of the most important tools that you will use in Indian cooking. I use one to coarsely or finely grind dry whole spices. It grinds them in seconds and clean up is very simple.

Electric coffee grinders are ideally suited for grinding a wide range of spices, such as cumin seeds, cinnamon sticks (broken up), cardamom and bay leaves. They can grind as little as a teaspoon to as much as half a cup. Use a blender for larger volumes of whole spices. A spice grinder or coffee grinder will make your cooking process very simple and the results very flavorful. If you use a coffee grinder to grind spices, reserve it for that use only; otherwise, you will end up with cumin-flavored coffee.

Cast-Iron Skillets and Griddles

Small cast-iron skillets are ideal for dry roasting spices because they evenly brown them without needing to add any cooking fat or liquid. Always preheat your cast-iron pan before frying in it.

A large cast-iron skillet or griddle is excellent for making Indian flatbreads. Traditionally, these breads are cooked in a *tava*, a round, concave, cast-iron griddle that is available in South Asian grocery stores.

You can cook almost any food in cast-iron cookware, but new cast-iron pans should be seasoned before use according to the manufacturer's instructions. Cast iron is a natural non-stick surface if your pan is seasoned correctly, making it a great alternative to artificial non-stick cooking surfaces.

Cast-iron can be pre-heated to temperatures that will brown meat and will withstand oven temperatures well above what is considered safe for non-stick pans—just don't put cold liquid into a very hot cast-iron pan; doing so might damage or crack the pan.

indian ingredients

The following is a description of some of the most popular and commonly used ingredients in this book. Many of the ingredients and spices used in *Easy Indian Cooking* are found in well-stocked supermarkets. These include cumin, coriander, turmeric, black pepper, ginger, paprika, cayenne pepper, cloves, cinnamon and cardamom. Some others are carried in South Asian or Indian food markets. It is also possible to order spices by mail and on the internet. Indian cuisine has always been very compatible with spices and ingredients from other cuisines and cultures. I use a lot of ingredients that are locally available and not used in a traditional Indian kitchen. Olive oil is one of them. Even though in most cases Indian recipes call for any neutral-flavored vegetable oil (for example, canola, safflower or corn oil), olive oil is a healthier alternative. I often use it to drizzle over salads and sometimes for lighter cooking.

Storage Tips for Spices and Herbs

Ideally, it is best to buy all dry spices in their whole form. Whole spices will stay fresh generally five to six months longer than pre-ground spices. It's a good habit to smell ground spices before using them; if their smell is very faint, it's time to replace them or grind a fresh batch. Both whole and ground spices should be stored in a cool, dry, dark place in tightly covered jars. Freshly ground spices are not the same as pre-ground store-bought spices. Freshly ground spices are far superior in flavor and aroma to pre-ground spices. Another difference is in the weight and volume: freshly ground spices have less weight per tablespoon (or greater volume per ounce), than pre-ground spices, which settle over time. You might think you would need to use more of the freshly-ground spice to compensate for the greater density of the settled pre-ground spice. But because pre-ground spices are so much less potent than freshly ground, the difference in mass is not of consequence. If anything, you might need to add *more* of the pre-ground spice.

To prolong the life span of fresh herbs, like fresh coriander leaves (cilantro) and mint, wash and dry the leaves with a paper towel until the leaves are mostly dried. Store refrigerated, wrapped in a kitchen or paper towel, in a resealable plastic food storage bag.

Asian Chili Powder

This is a red powder made from grinding dried red skins of several types of chili peppers. In India, it is simply called "chili powder." You can substitute cayenne pepper, which is commonly available in supermarkets. The Indian chili powder, which is darker in color than cayenne pepper, is available in Indian grocery stores. It adds a spicy flavor to dishes.

When fresh, the leaves are very mild and do not develop their full flavor until several weeks after picking and drying. They are often used whole, or sometimes ground in curries and rice dishes. They are an important ingredient in the Indian spice blend garam masala. Bay leaves are also a common fixture in the cooking of many European cuisines (particularly those of the Mediterranean), as well as North and South American cuisines. The bay leaf that is commonly available in North America is similar in appearance to the Indian bay leaf, but its flavor and fragrance are milder than the Indian counterpart. If you cannot find Indian bay leaves, which are often found only in Indian grocery stores, you may substitute regular bay leaves. The difference is very subtle and will not affect the final result.

Bay Leaves

These are long, oval, pointed and smooth leaves of a hardy evergreen shrub. The leaves are dark green when fresh and turn olive green when dry.

Cardamom

The cardamom plant is native to India and Sri Lanka and is also cultivated in Guatemala, Mexico, Indonesia and other areas of southern Asia.

The cardamom pods are harvested just before they are ripe and they are allowed to dry in the sun or sometimes in drying machines. There are two distinct types of cardamom pods used in Indian cooking: the small green pod and large black pod. The green pods are the most common and have exceptional flavor. I recommend using the green pods whenever cardamom is called for in this book. Black cardamom pods are used in Indian rice and meat dishes; however, they are not as commonly available.

Cardamom pods are used in almost every part of the cuisine, from savory dishes to curries and desserts. When using cardamom for desserts, the seeds are extracted from the pods and ground to a powder. For curries, stews or rice dishes, the whole pod can be added directly to the food. The sharp and bitter taste of cardamom mellows to a warming sweet taste as it cooks. The preground preparation is more readily available than the pods in the West, whereas in India it is typical to find the whole pod. The quality of preground cardamom is not as good as that found when freshly grinding the seeds at home. Once the pods are opened or the seeds ground, the flavor and aroma of the cardamom are lost very quickly. I especially recommend freshly grinding the seeds for the dessert and beverage recipes, where the spice often plays a particularly prominent role.

Chili Peppers

There are more than 150 varieties of chili peppers in the world. That's a lot to keep track of, but as a general rule the smaller ones are hotter than the larger ones. The two most common chilies used in Indian cooking are the cayenne and Thai. The cayenne pepper is green when fresh and red when dried. The Thai variety, or "bird's eye," is smaller and hotter. The serrano chili is more widely available in the U.S. and is a good alternative to the cayenne and Thai, though it is milder. If you cannot find fresh cayenne, Thai or serrano chili peppers, simply use what's available.

Fresh Chilies These are one of the most important ingredients for providing pungency in Indian cuisine. In many regions in India fresh green chilies are served raw with the food. I often remove the inner membrane and seeds and use only the skin to reduce the heat. Chopping fresh chili releases capsaicin, and the finer you chop it, the hotter the taste. Sometimes I slit the chilies open, but leave the seeds intact to release a gentler heat.

Dried Red Chili Peppers Whole dried red hot chilies, about 1½ to 2 inches (4 to 5 cm) long, are usually added to hot oil to infuse their strong flavor. A quick contact with hot oil enhances and intensifies the flavor of the skins. Indian dried red chilies are similar to most common types such as the cayenne and chili de arbol.

Cinnamon

This fragrant spice is the dried inner bark of the laurel tree. It is an important ingredient in Indian cooking, imparting a pleasant aroma to foods. It is sold in powder and stick forms. Whole sticks are used to flavor meats, curry and rice dishes as well as teas.

Cloves

These are dried unopened buds of a tropical tree. Deep reddish brown cloves add a strong fragrance to rice and grain recipes. It is also an important ingredient in garam masala. The cloves are lightly fried in hot oil, which perfumes the food subsequently cooked in the oil.

Coconut Milk, Coconut Meat, Shredded Coconut

In my recipes I use coconut milk, coconut meat and shredded coconut. Coconut milk is produced by crushing the thick white coconut meat that is inside the dark brown coconut shell. Water is added to the macerated mixture. It is then drained and the soaked coconut meat is squeezed to extract the liquid. As the milk sits, the fat rises to the surface. This fat is skimmed off and sold separately as coconut cream. The cream is much richer and thicker than the milk. Coconut milk and coconut cream are both sold in cans. When using coconut milk for savory recipes, make sure it is not sweetened. Sweetened milk or cream is used in making pastries and cocktails. I prefer to used full-fat coconut milk rather than the "lite" version, which is not as flavorful or creamy. Before opening a can of coconut milk make sure to shake it well, as the cream will have risen to the top; shaking the can incorporates the cream into the thinner milk-like liquid to create a smooth, even consistency. Once the can is opened make sure you store it covered in the refrigerator and use it within 2 to 3 days, as it spoils quickly.

Packaged shredded coconut (sometimes called "grated") is available frozen, which is the next best option to freshly grated, and dried, or "desiccated." For the recipes in this book, be sure to purchase unsweetened shredded coconut. While dried unsweetened coconut is easy to find in most supermarkets or health food stores, frozen shredded coconut is available only in Southeast Asian or Indian grocery stores. The dried shredded coconut, however, has significantly less flavor than the frozen or fresh forms and does not give the creamy texture that is desired in Indian curries and stews. If you only have access to dried, unsweetened shredded coconut, soak ½ cup (50 g) of the dried coconut in ½ cup (125 ml) of boiling water for about 15 minutes. Drain the excess water before use. Note that ½ cup of dried coconut is comparable to 1 cup of freshly shredded or frozen shredded coconut.

Freshly shredded, or grated, coconut will provide the best flavor and texture in Indian dishes. This requires purchasing a coconut and whacking it apart at home. Here is how to grate fresh coconut at home: Start with a clean looking coconut without cracks or any overpowering or rancid smell. It should feel heavy and full of water. You can shake the coconut to hear the water swish. Place the coconut on a clean, heavy wooden cutting board or a clean concrete block. Holding the coconut in one hand, tap the coconut lightly on all sides with a hammer to dislodge the insides from the hard brown shell. Then carefully but forcefully hit the shell with the hammer to break it open. Now most of the hard shell should separate from the coconut. Carefully pry off the meat from the brown outer shell with the tip of a well rounded blunt knife. Grate the coconut meat using a handheld grater.

Coriander Leaves

Also known as "cilantro," the leaves of this plant, an annual in the parsley family, is one of the most commonly used herbs in Indian cuisine. This herb is generally used uncooked for garnishes, marinades and chutneys. Many dishes also incorporate fresh coriander leaves at various stages of cooking, which dissipates the sharp flavor and aroma of the herb, leaving a mild flavor. Fresh coriander leaves are highly perishable and prone to wilting. See "Storage Tips for Spices and Herbs," page 10.

Coriander Seeds

Coriander seeds are ribbed peppercorn-sized and -shaped pale green to light brown-colored seeds of the coriander (or cilantro) plant. They are extremely aromatic, with a spicy hint; yet, taste and aroma are in no way similar to the leaves of the coriander plant. I always keep them in small quantities in airtight containers, as they lose their flavor with exposure and age. Coriander seeds are also available in a pre-ground form.

Cucumbers

Cucumbers are widely used in Indian kitchens and can be served with any Indian meal. Cucumbers can always be found in my refrigerator and are a summertime favorite. The cooling, clean flavor matches well with foods like chilies, cilantro, cream, garlic, lemon, lime, mint, olive oil, onions, sour cream, tomatoes, vinegar and yogurt. I like to cut them into little finger sized wedges and serve it with a sprinkle of salt, black pepper, Asian chili powder or cayenne pepper and a heavy dose of fresh squeezed lemon juice.

When purchasing cucumbers, look for smooth, brightly-colored skin. Cucumbers keep well in a plastic bag in the refrigerator for up to ten days. I prefer to use the long seedless variety called "English" cucumbers. They are usually sold shrink wrapped and they aren't actually seedless—the seeds are just very small. These cucumbers can be eaten without peeling and seeding unlike the common, garden-variety salad cucumber.

Cumin Seeds

These seeds are the best-known and most widely used spice in Indian cuisine. They are either fried whole in hot oil or dry roasted and then used whole or finely ground, according to the recipe. Cumin is warm, intense, and has an almost nutty aroma.

Curry Leaves, Fresh and Dried

Curry leaves originate from the kari tree, a sub-tropical tree native to India. They are used similarly to the way bay leaves are used—mainly as an aromatic and flavoring for most curries and soups. They are widely used in dishes along the southern coastal regions of India. When starting a curry or soup dish, curry leaves are placed in hot oil to fry until crisp, which makes the oil and the leaves intensely flavorful. It is common to use fresh curry leaves in India rather than dried. You can purchase fresh curry leaves in Indian grocery stores. Dried curry leaves can be purchased from specialty gourmet stores or online. The best way to store fresh curry leaves is to wash and pat them mostly dry with a paper towel. Store refrigerated, wrapped in a kitchen towel or a paper towel in a resealable food storage bag. They will stay fresh for up to a month. For extended use, air dry them completely and store in an airtight container.

Dried Legumes (Lentils, Dried Beans and Peas)

In India, all types of dried legumes, be they lentils, peas or beans, are known as *dals*. They are an integral part of Indian meals, being economical, highly nutritious, very low in fat and a good source of carbohydrates, proteins, fibers, minerals and vitamins. *Dals* are a good substitute for meat, which has more fat and cholesterol. Many common varieties of *dals*, like chickpeas (*kabuli chana*), kidney beans (*rajmah*), whole green lentils (*sabut moong*) and cow peas (black-eyed peas), are available in conventional supermarket. Some not-so-common varieties that are used in Indian cooking include pigeon peas (*toor dal*), split black *gram*, aka "black lentils" (*urad dal*), split green lentils (*moong dal*), split red lentils (*masoor dal*) and yellow split peas (*chana dal*). To procure these, a trip to an Indian grocery store or an online purchase is necessary. I often stock my pantry with canned legumes, which I find to be an acceptable substitute for dried and very convenient to use when I'm in a rush. In the *dal* recipes in this book, I include the option of using commonly available canned peas or beans. Make sure to drain and rinse them thoroughly before using them.

From top to bottom: *split yellow peas* (chana dal) *and mung beans (*mung dal*), split red lentils (*masoor dal*), split pigeon peas (*toor dal*) and black-eyed peas.*

Fennel Seeds

These are the oval pale greenish-yellow seeds of the common fennel plant, a member of parsley family. They are sweetly aromatic and have an aniselike flavor. In Indian cooking, they are used whole and ground in both sweet and savory dishes. Roasted fennel seeds are sometimes sugarcoated and chewed as a digestive and mouth freshener after Indian meals. They are available most grocery stores.

Fenugreek Seeds

Fenugreek seeds are tiny, bitter, yellowish-brown seeds that provide commercial curry powders with their distinctive aroma. They are used in small quantities because of their strong flavor. The seeds are often oil-roasted and then ground to create a bitter balance in curries in the southern part of India; in the eastern part of India the seeds are stir-fried whole. Whole fenugreek seeds are available only in Southeast Asian or Indian grocery stores.

Garlic

A close relative to onion, shallot and the leek, garlic has been used throughout recorded history for both culinary and medicinal purposes. It has a characteristic pungent, spicy flavor that mellows and sweetens considerably with cooking. Garlic powder is not a substitute for fresh garlic in traditional Indian cooking. Whole bulbs of garlic will keep for several months or longer when stored at room temperature in a dry, dark place that has ample air circulation. Keep in mind, however, that garlic's shelf life begins to decrease more rapidly once you start removing cloves from the bulb. Storing garlic uncovered, such as in a wire-mesh basket inside your cupboard is ideal. You can also store garlic in a paper bag or a mesh bag. Just be sure there is plenty of dry air and little light to inhibit sprouting. To avoid mold, do not refrigerate or store garlic in plastic bags.

Ginger

Ginger is a knobby, pale-brown rhizome of a perennial tropical plant. It is available fresh, dried and ground into a powder and as a preserved stem. Ground ginger or preserved ginger is almost never used in Indian cooking. Fresh ginger root has no aroma, but once you peel or cut it, it emits a warm, woody aroma with citrus undertones. When used fresh, it has a peppery hot bite to it. Fresh ginger is used throughout India and is a very common ingredient in Indian cooking. It is often ground into a paste, finely chopped, or made into juice. We add chopped ginger to stir-fry vegetables, crushed ginger or ginger paste in meat stews and legumes and thinly sliced slivers of raw ginger are sometimes sprinkled over curries just before serving. While shopping for fresh ginger, look for a hard and heavy root that snaps easily into pieces. Avoid dry, shriveled roots that feel light for their size. Keep fresh ginger in your refrigerator crisper in a plastic bag with a paper towel to absorb moisture (to prevent mold, change the towel occasionally). It will last for two or three weeks. To extend its life, you can freeze ginger. You don't even need to defrost it, and ginger is much easier to grate when frozen.

Lentils
see **Dried Legumes**

Mace

Mace is the dark, red, lacy membrane that covers the outside of the nutmeg shell. This is skillfully removed after the fruit bursts opens, then flattened and dried to become mace, as we know the spice. Mace has a rich, warm, citrusy, spicy aroma and bitter taste, very similar to nutmeg, only stronger. It is often used in small quantities for making spice blends and pastes. Whole mace, or "blades," is often toasted and ground and then mixed with yogurt, herbs and other spices to marinate Indian grilled or roasted meats. Whole mace is also an important ingredient in rice dishes made with basmati rice, such as Saffron Rice and Chicken Casserole (page 81), where it imparts a unique flavor to the dish. This aromatic spice is a delightful match for the wonderful fragrance of basmati rice. Whole mace is available in Indian or Middle Eastern grocery stores or online.

Mint

Mint is an aromatic, almost exclusively perennial herb with a very refreshing taste. Fresh mint is often used in Indian marinades, chutneys, drinks and desserts, as well as in certain curries and rice dishes. I also use dried mint for making breads in my kitchen. Chopped fresh mint leaves steeped in a cup of hot water with tea and honey is one of my favorite soothing after-dinner digestif

beverages. The spearmint variety is most commonly used in Indian cooking. When purchasing mint, make sure the leaves are fresh and green in color without and black spots or cracks. See "Storage Tips for Spices and Herbs," page 10.

Mustard Seeds

These tiny, round, hot and pungent seeds are from an annual plant of the cabbage family. They are available in white, yellow, brown, or black colors. The white seeds, the largest type, are used to make commercial mustards in the United States; and the yellow and brown seeds are used for European mustards and for pickling. In India, the black seeds are used in cooking and are the source of commonly used oil. Black mustard seeds are used whole and in powdered form. The whole seeds are used in vegetable dishes, curries, appetizers, salads, and dried legumes, while the powder is used to flavor steamed fish, pickles, and, again, curries. Mustard seeds are available at Indian grocery stores and online.

Oils and Fats

In Indian kitchens, oil is used alone or in combination with *ghee* (clarified butter) to fry flavorings at the start of cooking or to deep-fry foods. The oil used depends on the culture and region. When I call for oil, you many use any neutral-flavored vegetable oil (for example, canola, safflower or corn oil). In addition to using unflavored oils, Indians use toasted sesame oil, coconut oil, peanut and mustard oil to impart distinct flavors to dishes. I have not used these oils in my recipes as some are hard to find and they give a very distinct flavor to the food, which, though popular in India, can be an acquired taste for non-Indian. When I call for oil for deep-frying, it's important to use an oil that is relatively stable at high temperatures, such as peanut oil or safflower oil. Additionally, olive oil, which is a very healthy oil, can also be used to cook Indian food.

Paprika

Known as *Kashmiri mirch* in India, paprika is a red powder made from

dried, mild, non-pungent chili peppers. It is mainly used for the rich red color it adds to curries. When added to hot oil, it immediately releases a deep red color. Most Indian paprika comes from Kashmir, hence the name. *Kashmiri mirch* is available at Indian grocery stores or online. The easily available, mild Hungarian paprika is a good substitute.

Peppercorns

Peppercorns range in color from white, green to black. White peppercorns are picked ripe, and their outer skin is removed. Green peppercorns are under-ripe berries that are cured in brine. Black peppercorns are picked under ripe and allowed to dry until dark black. Black peppercorns are most commonly used and impart an incredible flavor to all curries. The world's top quality black pepper is grown in Indian in the southwest coastal state of Kerala, and is known as *Tellicherry pepper*. The recipes in this book call for dry and oil-roasted, ground and crushed black peppercorns.

Pulses
see **Dried Legumes**

Rice

Rice is an indispensible part of Indian meals. It is served as a staple alongside curries and dals and is eaten at least twice a day in India. There are many distinctive kinds of rice grown and sold in the Indian subcontinent. For everyday meals, the type of rice used depends varies from region to region. While the people in southern regions prefer the locally available red rice or long-grain variety, northerners prefer the aromatic Basmati rice, which grows in the foothills of the Himalayas.

Basmati, which means "queen of fragrance" in Hindi, is the most popular and the best-known rice of India, and it is the most expensive. It has a wonderful fragrance when cooked with whole spices and is a good match for all Indian dishes. Basmati rice is always used for *pulaos* and *biryanis*—two types of rice dishes—for it absorbs flavors beautifully and

yet keeps its shape during cooking. Basmati rice, though preferred, is not absolutely necessary when making simpler rice preparations, such as Rosemary Lemon Rice (page 74) or Mint Pilaf with Potatoes and Toasted Cumin (page 78). Whereas Basmati rice needs to be soaked prior to being rinsed and drained, ordinary long-grain rice only needs to be rinsed and drained.

Saffron

These intense yellow-orange threads are the dried orange-to-deep-red stigmas of a small purple flower of the saffron crocus, a member of the iris family. It is the world's most expensive spice as it takes almost 75,000 handpicked blossoms to make one pound of saffron. Use saffron sparingly as it just takes four to five strands of saffron to flavor a dish that feeds four. It has a distinctly warm, rich, powerful and intense flavor. It is available in strands or ground. I recommend the strands for the sake of more assured quality. Gently heat

saffron on a dry skillet before using as heat brings out its aroma. There is no acceptable substitute for saffron. Saffron is available in Indian or Middle Eastern grocery stores, gourmet stores and online.

Salt

The most common salt that is used in North America is table salt. It is very fine in texture and is often supplemented with iodine. Table salt, when compared to kosher or sea salt, is much saltier. Sea salt is the most popular salt used in Indian cooking. Measurements used in the recipes in this book are for common table salt. If you prefer to use kosher salt or sea salt, you will most likely need to increase the amount of salt by 10 to 15 percent. However, it is always a good idea to taste and check for seasoning before adding more.

Sesame Seeds

These tiny seeds are harvested from a flowering plant found in tropical regions around the world and is culti-

vated for its edible seeds. Whole or ground white sesame seeds are used in savory Indian dishes, breads and many sweets. Sometimes the seeds are toasted to heighten their nutty flavor. They come in a host of different colors, depending upon the variety, including white, yellow, black and red. In general, the paler varieties of sesame are used in the West and Middle East, while the black varieties are more common in the East. They are available in most grocery stores.

Star Anise

This dried, star-shaped, dark-brown pod contains licorice-flavored seeds. The pods grow on an evergreen tree that is a member of the magnolia family. Star anise is used to flavor and add an enticing aroma to both sweet and savory dishes. It is often used on its own or ground with different spices to make blends. This spice is available at Indian and Asian grocery stores, online and at many conventional supermarkets.

Tamarind

Tamarind is the curved brown bean pod of the tamarind tree. The pod contains a sticky pulp enclosing one to twelve shiny black seeds. It is the pulp that is used as a flavoring for its sweet-and-sour fruity aroma and taste. It is used in chutneys, preserves and curries. Tamarind is available in South Asian grocery stores, natural foods stores, and some conventional supermarkets in one or more of the following three ways: in pod form, pressed into a fibrous dried slab, or in jars of tamarind "paste" or "concentrate," which has a jam-like consistency. I call for the tamarind paste in the recipes in this book simply because it is the most convenient form to use and is fairly easy to find.

Alternatively to create tamarind juice from the dried slab, soak a walnut-size chunk of the dried pulp (this is equivalent to 1 teaspoon of tamarind paste) in ½ cup (125 ml) of warm water for 15 minutes. After soaking the pulp in water, break it up with your fingers, and then mash it with a fork until the liquid is muddy brown in appearance. Strain this mixture before use through a fine-mesh strainer. Using the back of spoon, mash and push the pulp through the fine-mesh strainer to extract any remaining juice.

Turmeric

It is a rhizome of a tropical plant in the ginger family. The fresh root is boiled, peeled, sun-dried, and ground into a bright yellow-orange powder. Ground turmeric has a warm, peppery aroma—reminiscent of ginger—and a strong, bitter taste, which mellows upon cooking. It is used to color many curries and is sometimes used as a "poor man's substitute" for saffron due to the similar color it imparts; however, the taste is quite different.

Yogurt

Thick and creamy yogurt is made every day in homes across the Indian subcontinent and it is an important part of every meal. It is most commonly enjoyed plain as a mild contrast to spicy foods. *Raitas*—cooling salads made with yogurt and crunchy vegetables—are very popular. Yogurt is often churned into cooling drinks with spices, and is the base for many desserts. In savory cooking, its main role is as a souring agent, though it also aids digestion. In India it is customary to end a meal with either plain yogurt mixed with rice or a glass of Indian spiced "buttermilk" (thinned yogurt with salt, green chilies, ginger and salt which is common in south India). The best yogurt to use for the recipes in this book is a thick, plain, natural yogurt made from whole milk. Look for organic whole milk yogurt for the best consistency and flavor.

accompaniments

 They don't call them "accompaniments" for nothing! These sauces and dips add that little "something extra" to every bite of a meal. When we are hungry, we eat not only to fill our bellies; we eat so that we can savor a combination of flavors that satisfy our taste buds. That's where these accompaniments step in. They are usually made with fruits or vegetables, and are often flavored with sugar, vinegar, yogurt or a blend of different spices. They can be made into pastes, like *sambal*, and enjoyed with rice-based main courses; or have the consistency of a thin dipping sauce, like *chutney*, which works as a perfect accompaniment for *samosas*, which are stuffed and fried turnovers. Then there are the *raitas*—the most common and popular Indian accompaniment—a delectable cross between a sauce and a dip that act as a coolant for curries and other fiery-hot Indian dishes. Some accompaniments are made with crushed fruits or vegetables and can contain a marriage of different flavors. Some are even cooked, and their spices tempered, to give them a different dimension.

No Indian meal is complete without at least one accompaniment, and fancy meals may have as many as five or more. Throughout this chapter, I suggest classic pairings for these accompaniments, but please don't rely on my taste buds alone. I urge you to trust your culinary instincts and try experimenting with seasonal fresh fruit or produce, and basic spices and herbs that are readily available at your favorite local grocery store. Often, the results are surprising and good.

In India, chutneys are usually freshly made each day because they contain no preservatives. I often make them in batches and refrigerate or freeze them for those times when I need that extra bit of flavor to zing up my menu.

potato raita with chives and cumin

Serves 4   Preparation 10 minutes   Cooking 30 minutes

If there ever was a staple accompaniment on the Indian table, it is raita. Various vegetables, sometimes cooked, sometimes raw, are used in making raitas. Here, I have added chives for a flavor that's slightly different than the run-of-the-mill raita. Enjoy this with Spinach and Thyme Roti Flatbreads (page 76).

1 large potato or 2 medium potatoes (½ lb/225 g), scrubbed clean with a brush
2½ cups (610 g) plain yogurt, whisked until smooth
Salt, to taste
2 teaspoons cumin seeds, toasted and ground
1 teaspoon black peppercorns, toasted and ground
½ cup (16 g) minced chives
½ red bell pepper, deseeded and finely chopped

1 Peel the potato before or after cooking. Place the potato in a pan, cover with lightly salted water, and boil until tender, about 25–30 minutes. Drain. (Alternatively, you can fork-perforate and microwave the potato for 4–8 minutes.) When cool enough to handle, cut the peeled potato into 1-in (2.5-cm) dice.

2 Place the yogurt in a serving bowl, mix in the potato, salt, and half of the ground cumin seed and peppercorns. Add the chives and red bell pepper. Garnish with the remaining ground spices, and serve.

spiced hummus with almonds

Makes 3 cups (800 g)   Preparation 10 minutes

Dried or canned chickpeas are a basic item in any Indian pantry. For this dip, you can use canned garbanzo beans, which are also called chickpeas. The addition of Indian spices makes this recipe delightful, and—when used as a dip for finger snacks, plain tortilla chips, or potato chips— it is an unusually easy-to-pull-off appetizer for your guests when you are in no particular mood to spend hours in the kitchen!

2 tablespoons sesame seeds
2 teaspoons ground cumin
1 cup (140 g) sliced almonds
2 cups (300 g) rinsed and drained garbanzo beans (chickpeas) from one 19-oz (583-g) can
5 cloves garlic, chopped
¼ cup (2 g) fresh mint leaves
¼ cup (65 ml) fresh lemon juice
1 teaspoon sugar
Salt, to taste
½ teaspoon freshly-ground black pepper
1 teaspoon prepared garam masala

1 Toast the sesame seeds in a dry skillet on medium heat until slightly toasted and brown, about a minute. Set aside.

2 Toast the cumin seeds in a dry skillet on medium heat until slightly toasted and brown, about a minute. Set aside.

3 Blend the almonds, garbanzo beans, sesame seeds, and garlic with a little water in a blender or food processor to make a smooth paste.

4 Add the mint, lemon juice, sugar, salt, pepper, cumin and garam masala, and blend. Serve cold as a dipping sauce.

wasabi and green chili chutney

Makes **1 cup (300 g)**   Preparation **10 minutes**

Don't let the words "wasabi" or "green chili" scare you away from this chutney. The mayonnaise and lime juice cut through the heat of these immensely spicy ingredients to give you a dip that isn't too dangerous for your palate. Enjoy this spread on basic vegetable sandwiches or smeared on a plain flatbread or Potato and Dill Stuffed Parathas (page 74).

1 tablespoon prepared wasabi paste
2 small fresh green chili peppers, deseeded
5 green onions (scallions), coarsely chopped
1 cup (8 g) fresh mint leaves
3 cups (120 g) coarsely-chopped fresh coriander leaves (cilantro)
¼ cup (65 ml) fresh lime juice
1 tablespoon low-fat mayonnaise
2 teaspoons sugar
Salt, to taste

1 Blend the wasabi, green chili peppers and green onions in a blender or food processor until well minced. Add the mint and coriander leaves, and then continue blending, scraping the sides with a spatula, until puréed. As you blend, drizzle the lime juice through the feeder tube into the bowl and process until the chutney is smooth.
2 Add the mayonnaise, sugar and salt, and mix. Adjust the seasonings. Transfer to a bowl and serve immediately or refrigerate for up to two weeks.

coconut and red chili sambal

Makes **2 cups (800 g)**   Preparation **10 minutes**   Cooking **5 minutes**

Sambal is a common table condiment in South Indian households. Adjust the number of red chili peppers that you use at your discretion, as prepared sambal chili paste is quite spicy on its own. Sambal chili paste is found in most Asian markets in the United States. Serve it on the side with Crispy Southern Indian Fried Fish (page 66) or Goan Crab Cakes (page 63).

3 cups (500 g) shredded, unsweetened coconut (frozen, reconstituted dried or freshly grated)
2–3 dried red chili peppers, to taste
1 tablespoon prepared sambal chili paste
2-in (5-cm) piece peeled and sliced fresh ginger
3 tablespoons fresh lemon juice
1 cup (250 g) plain yogurt
1 cup (40 g) coarsely-chopped fresh coriander leaves (cilantro)
Salt, to taste

Garnish
1 tablespoon oil
1 teaspoon black mustard seeds
2 tablespoons minced fresh curry leaves

1 Blend the coconut, red chili peppers, sambal chili paste and ginger in a blender or food processor until minced.
2 Add the lemon juice, yogurt, and fresh coriander leaves, and blend again, scraping the mixture from the sides with a spatula until it becomes very smooth. Add the salt and transfer to a serving bowl.
3 Make the garnish: heat the oil in a small non-stick saucepan over medium-high heat and add the mustard seeds and curry leaves. Lower the heat and cover until the spluttering subsides. Add to the sambal and stir lightly. Serve, or refrigerate for up to 2 weeks.

sweet cranberry and lemon chutney

Makes **3 cups (800 g)**   Preparation **10 minutes**   Cooking **40 minutes**

On the West Coast, Meyer lemons are almost a staple at farmers' markets. They've become so popular that they are now available in grocery stores in most parts of the United States. I personally love the aroma of this variety of lemon, and hence use it a lot—especially during Thanksgiving!

1 tablespoon oil
1 cinnamon stick
2 star anise pods
3 cloves
2 tablespoons fennel seeds
2 tablespoons peeled and minced fresh ginger
1 lb (500 g) fresh cranberries
Grated zest from 5 Meyer or regular lemons
Juice of 2 Meyer or regular lemons
2 cups (400 g) sugar
6 cups (1.5 liters) water
Pinch of saffron threads
Salt, to taste
3 tablespoons red wine vinegar

1 Heat the oil in a large saucepan over medium-high heat and cook the cinnamon, star anise pods, cloves, fennel seeds and ginger, stirring for about 30 seconds.

2 Add the cranberries, lemon zest, lemon juice, sugar, water, saffron and salt, and bring to a boil over high heat. Boil, stirring occasionally, until the mixture is slightly thickened, about 15 to 20 minutes.

3 Reduce the heat to medium, add the vinegar, and cook until the mixture thickens to a jam-like consistency, about 10 minutes. Transfer to a bowl, let cool, and serve at room temperature, or refrigerate at least 2 hours and serve chilled. It can be stored in an airtight container in the refrigerator for up to 3 months.

pomegranate mint chutney

Makes **1 cup (250 g)**   Preparation **10 minutes**

Mint chutney is the most popular chutney in India. Every household adds its own special touches, and there are hundreds of variations. If you find dried pomegranate seeds at the Indian grocery store, add a teaspoon of them to this recipe to add great flavor. This chutney goes well with any Indian snacks, breads, or grilled meats and poultry, and can be refrigerated for up to a week or frozen for two to three months.

1 small red onion, coarsely chopped
2 fresh green chili peppers, deseeded and chopped
1 tablespoon fresh lemon juice
4 tablespoons water
4 cups (32 g) fresh mint leaves
1 cup (40 g) coarsely-chopped fresh coriander leaves (cilantro)
1 cup (180 g) fresh pomegranate seeds
1 teaspoon sugar
Salt, to taste
2 tablespoons fresh pomegranate seeds, for garnish

1 Add the red onion, green chili peppers, lemon juice and 2 tablespoons of the water to a blender or food processor, and blend until smooth. Add the mint and coriander leaves, and continue blending until smooth. Add the remaining 2 tablespoons of water, if needed.

2 Add the pomegranate seeds (reserve a few for garnishing), sugar and salt, and blend again. Adjust the seasonings. Transfer to a bowl and serve immediately or refrigerate. Garnish with fresh pomegranate seeds.

pan-roasted eggplant pachadi dip with sesame

Serves **4**   Preparation **10 minutes**   Cooking **15 minutes**

This is one of my favorite dips as it goes well with many dishes. This dish can also be made with left over Oven-Roasted Spiced Eggplant (page 95). Simply mix a cup of eggplant into 2 cups of beaten yogurt. Serve this delicious accompaniment with Potato and Dill Stuffed Parathas (page 74) or as a side with a wholesome rice dish like Saffron Rice and Chicken Casserole (page 81).

1 tablespoon sesame seeds
1 tablespoon vegetable oil
1 teaspoon minced garlic
1 small red onion, minced
1 small eggplant (½ lb/225 g), cut into 1-in (2.5-cm) pieces
1 red bell pepper, roasted (page 8)
3 cups (740 g) plain yogurt, whisked until smooth
Salt, to taste
1 teaspoon sesame oil

1 Toast the sesame seeds in a dry skillet on a medium heat until slightly toasted and brown, about a minute. Set aside.
2 Heat the vegetable oil in a large saucepan over medium-high heat. Add the garlic and onion and cook, stirring until golden, about 1 minute. Add the eggplant and cook, stirring until golden brown, about 5 to 10 minutes. Cover the pan and cook over low heat until the eggplant pieces are very soft, about 5 minutes. Let the eggplant cool in the pan.
3 Remove the charred skin from the roasted bell pepper. Deseed it and dice half of it. Set aside.
4 Place the yogurt in a serving bowl. Add the salt and mix in the cooled eggplant with the pan drippings. Serve garnished with the sesame oil and seeds, and diced bell pepper.

plum tomato mustard dip

Makes **1 cup (400 g)**   Preparation **15 minutes**   Cooking **10 minutes**

I like to think of this as Indian salsa. Tempered with curry leaves and mustard seeds, it is a tangy, sweet and Indianized tomato-based dip that is delicious with chips.

1 tablespoon coriander seeds
1 teaspoon cumin seeds
½ teaspoon black peppercorns
¼ cup (65 ml) oil
2 teaspoons black mustard seeds
1 teaspoon minced fresh curry leaves
2–3 dried red chili peppers, whole
2 large cloves garlic, minced
½ cup (75 g) minced red onion
1 teaspoon paprika
Salt, to taste
1 large plum tomato, chopped
2 tablespoons tomato paste
2 tablespoons white vinegar
¼ cup (65 ml) water

1 Grind the coriander seeds, cumin seeds and peppercorns in a spice or coffee grinder to make fine powder.
2 Heat the oil in a small saucepan over medium heat and add the mustard seeds, curry leaves and chili peppers. Lower the heat and cover the pan until the spluttering subsides. Add the garlic and onion, stir a few seconds, and then add the ground spices from step 1, paprika and salt, and cook, stirring for another 2 minutes.
3 Add the chopped tomato, tomato paste, vinegar and water, and cover the pan; reduce the heat to low and cook, stirring occasionally until the chutney is thick and fragrant, about 10 to 15 minutes. For the right consistency, it should be reduced to about 1 cup (400 g). Serve hot or cold.

mango and roasted red pepper chutney

Makes **2 cups (600 g)**   Preparation **10 minutes**   Cooking **30 minutes**

Mangoes are only available fresh when in season, but frozen mango slices also work well for this recipe. The sweetness and subtle pungency of this accompaniment is great with meat and poultry dishes like Lemon Pepper Chicken with Fresh Mint (page 40).

1 red bell pepper, roasted (page 8)
2 large mangoes (about 2 lbs/1 kg), peeled, pitted and diced
½ cup (125 ml) white balsamic vinegar or white wine vinegar
¼ cup (65 ml) honey
¼ cup (35 g) dried cherries
Salt, to taste
2 tablespoons oil
1 medium onion, chopped
1-in (2.5-cm) piece peeled and minced fresh ginger
3 cloves garlic, minced
1 teaspoon ground cumin
1 teaspoon ground coriander
1 teaspoon Asian chili powder or ground cayenne pepper

1 Remove the charred skin from the roasted bell pepper, then deseed and dice it. Set aside.
2 Toss together the mangoes, balsamic vinegar, honey, cherries and salt in a bowl. Set aside.
3 Sauté the onion with the oil in a medium saucepan over medium heat, stirring occasionally until cooked, 5–7 minutes.
4 Add the ginger, garlic, cumin, coriander and chili powder. Reduce the heat to low and cook, stirring for about 1 minute.
5 Stir in the mango mixture and simmer, stirring occasionally until the mangoes are tender, about 15 to 20 minutes. (Frozen mango pieces will become tender quicker.) Add the diced bell pepper and cook for 1 minute. Transfer to a serving bowl and let cool. Chill and serve cold.

beet and pineapple raita

Serves **4**   Preparation **10 minutes**   Cooking **15 minutes**

The great thing about raitas is that there isn't a set list of ingredients. Here I have used cooked diced beets with chunks of fresh pineapple that give it a citrus touch. But you can use any canned fruit or diced soft or cooked vegetables to make raita—just make sure you choose ingredients that create a balance of sweetness from the fruit and tartness from the yogurt.

2 medium beets, about ½ lb (225 g)
2 cups (500 g) plain yogurt, whisked until smooth
1 cup (250 g) sour cream, whisked until smooth
8 oz (250 g) peeled and cored fresh or canned pineapple, diced to ½-in (1.25-cm) pieces
5 green onions (scallions), minced
1 teaspoon garlic powder
1 small fresh green chili peppers, minced
Salt, to taste
½ teaspoon freshly-ground black pepper
2 tablespoons chopped fresh coriander leaves (cilantro)

1 Peel the beets before or after cooking. Place the beets in a small pan with water to cover by 2 in (5 cm) and bring to a boil over high heat. Reduce the heat to medium-low, cover, and simmer until tender, about 15 minutes. (Alternatively, pierce beets, place in 2 in (5 cm) of water, cover and microwave for 6–9 minutes.) Drain and when cool enough to handle, dice peeled beets to about ½ in (1.25 cm). Set aside to cool completely.
2 Mix the yogurt and sour cream together in a serving bowl. Add the cooked beets, pineapple, green onions, garlic powder, chili pepper, salt and black pepper, and stir to blend. Garnish with the fresh coriander leaves and serve.

appetizers, soups and salads

 Indians tend to be very social and gather around a rich array of snacking options, which includes appetizers, soups and salads. Many of these are spicy in taste and are comparatively lower in fat than most Western equivalents. Indian appetizers may be served with mint, fresh coriander (cilantro), tamarind, coconut chutney or any of the accompaniments included in this book.

In an everyday Indian home, salads are a very simple affair. A few basic fresh vegetables—like carrots, cucumbers, tomatoes and onions—are sliced or chopped, dressed with salt, pepper and lemon juice, and served alongside the meal. Feel free to mix fresh seasonal fruits and vegetables with a homemade dressing made of yogurt, lemon juice and freshly-ground Indian spices.

Indian soups are prepared differently than their Western counterparts. For example, Indian soups are almost never thickened with starch. The delicate use of spices, like cumin seeds, in combination with a moderate amount of green chili peppers, fresh herbs, lentils and vegetables imparts special aromas to these soups and makes them a perfect match for Indian fare. Some parts of India have extreme winter conditions, and some soups—especially the ones that contain aromatics and spices like ginger, cinnamon, and peppercorn—are meant to combat that chill. Most of these would also make a delicious and substantial lunchtime meal, perhaps served with some Indian bread, such as Fresh-Baked Rosemary Naan (page 75).

The soups in this chapter are easy to prepare and most can be made ahead of time and reheated just before serving. You can use a blender or a food processor to prepare them, and make their consistency as thick or thin as you like.

grilled chicken wings with ginger and lemon

Serves 4   Preparation 10 minutes   Cooking 15 minutes

A simple yet delicious grilled chicken dish that always gets raves from the health conscious! Yogurt, used instead of cream or mayonnaise in the marinade, adds taste without adding extra calories. Serve this with an accompaniment like Wasabi and Green Chili Chutney (page 20).

8 whole chicken wings, about 2 lbs (1 kg)

Spiced Yogurt Marinade
1 cup (245 g) plain yogurt, whisked until smooth
1 tablespoon ground cumin
1 tablespoon garam masala
1 teaspoon Asian chili powder or ground cayenne pepper
4-in (10-cm) piece peeled and minced fresh ginger
Salt, to taste
Juice of 2 lemons
8 cloves garlic, finely chopped

1 Remove the tips of the wings and discard. Use kitchen shears or a knife to separate the wings at the joint.

2 To make the Spiced Yogurt Marinade, mix together the yogurt, cumin, garam masala, chili powder, ginger, salt, lemon juice and garlic in a large bowl.

3 Add the chicken wings to the marinade and toss to evenly coat. Cover and refrigerate for 2 to 3 hours.

4 Preheat a grill pan or an indoor electric grill to high heat.

5 Place the chicken wings on the lightly-oiled hot grill in a single layer and cook for 5 or 6 minutes on each side, until the meat is charred at the edges, firm and completely cooked. Serve hot.

curry corn chowder with roasted poblanos

Serves 4   Preparation 10 minutes   Cooking 35 minutes

This innovative twist on corn chowder is hearty enough to be a meal on its own. Roasted and chopped poblano peppers add a nice chunky texture to the chowder, while curry powder and celery provide a unique and piquant taste.

2 poblano peppers

1 lb (500 g) potatoes, peeled and cut into 1-in (2.5-cm) cubes

¼ cup (65 ml) oil

1 teaspoon cumin seeds

1 onion, chopped

¼ cup (25 g) diced celery

½ cup (90 g) diced green bell pepper

Salt, to taste

3 cups (525 g) fresh corn kernels or thawed frozen corn

2 cups (500 ml) vegetable stock or water

1 cup (250 ml) heavy cream

1 tablespoon curry powder

3 tablespoons chopped fresh coriander leaves (cilantro)

1 Preheat the grill or a broiler to medium high heat.

2 Grill or broil the poblanos until the skin begins to blacken, 5 to 7 minutes. Transfer to a bowl, cover with plastic wrap, and let steam until the skin loosens, about 10 minutes. Peel the poblanos and coarsely chop. Set aside.

3 Add the potatoes to a small saucepan with enough water to cover, and cook until tender, 15 to 20 minutes. Drain and set aside.

4 Heat the oil in a large saucepan over medium high heat, then add the cumin, onion, celery and bell pepper, and sauté until the vegetables are softened, about 5 minutes. Add the salt and corn and cook for 3 to 4 minutes longer. Stir in the poblanos, potatoes, stock, heavy cream, curry powder and 1 tablespoon of the chopped coriander, and simmer until the soup thickens, 20 to 25 minutes.

5 Serve hot and garnish with the remaining chopped coriander.

mung bean and spinach samosa

Serves 6   Preparation 10 minutes   Cooking 5 minutes

This can be made with almost any pulse or dry cooked lentils leftovers. I have used mung beans, a staple in most Indian homes. Enveloped in layers of phyllo pastry sheets, these triangle-shaped turnovers are reminiscent of the ever-popular samosa, but baked rather than fried.

2 tablespoons oil
1 teaspoon cumin seeds
1½ tablespoons minced ginger
1 fresh green chili pepper, deseeded and minced
1 tablespoon ground coriander seeds
1¼ cups (185 g) dried mung beans, washed, soaked and drained
¼ teaspoon ground turmeric
Salt, to taste
1 cup (250 ml) water
1 cup (100 g) chopped fresh spinach
6 phyllo pastry sheets
2 tablespoons melted butter
1 egg, whisked for glaze

1 Heat the oil in a large non-stick saucepan over medium heat and add the cumin seeds, ginger, chili pepper and coriander. Stir for about 30 seconds. Mix in the mung beans, turmeric and salt, and stir for about 2 minutes.

2 Add the water and lower the heat to medium-low. Cover and cook until all the water has been absorbed and the mung beans are soft, about 10 to 15 minutes. Add the spinach and stir until wilted, about 1 minute. Cool the mixture.

3 Preheat the oven to 350°F (175°C).

4 Brush each phyllo sheet with the melted butter and stack them. Cut lengthwise with a sharp knife into 4 equal strips, each about 3 in (7.5 cm) wide. Stack again and cover with a clean damp kitchen towel. Cut each strip into 6 squares.

5 Place a phyllo strip lengthwise in front of you on a work surface and spoon a generous tablespoon of the filling into the center. Brush all around the edges of each with the egg glaze. Fold the right corner over the filling to the left side to make a triangle. Repeat with the rest of the phyllo strips and filling to make more turnovers.

6 Place the turnovers on a baking sheet and brush with the egg glaze. Bake until crisp and golden, about 20 minutes. Transfer to cooling racks.

7 Serve warm or at room temperature.

crispy pan-fried shrimp with tamarind glaze

Serves 6   Preparation 10 minutes   Cooking 10 minutes

Not surprisingly, this dish is by far one of the fastest moving at Indian restaurants. Here I have used Thai basil to give it an interesting twist. If you can't find Thai basil, substitute regular basil. The flavors of the basil, tamarind and spices marry beautifully, and sooner than later, you'll find this dish among your favorites too. Besides tasting great, the real beauty of this dish is its simplicity, making it possible to conjure it up in a jiffy.

1 lb (500 g) medium size fresh shrimp, shelled, de-veined and rinsed
2 tablespoons oil, for frying
Juice of 1 lemon
2 tablespoons chopped fresh Thai basil

Spicy Tamarind Marinade
1 teaspoon peeled and minced fresh ginger
4 teaspoons minced garlic
1 teaspoon ground cumin
1 tablespoon tamarind paste
1 teaspoon Asian chili powder or ground cayenne pepper
½ teaspoon ground turmeric
1 tablespoon all-purpose flour
Salt, to taste
2 tablespoons oil

1 Pat the shrimp dry with a clean kitchen towel and set aside.

2 Prepare the Spicy Tamarind Marinade: Mix the ginger and garlic with the cumin in a large bowl. Add the tamarind paste, chili powder, turmeric, flour and salt. Stir the oil into the mixture.

3 Add the shrimp to the bowl with the marinade and toss well to coat evenly. Cover and refrigerate for about 2 hours.

4 Heat the 2 tablespoons of oil in a large saucepan over medium heat. Add the marinated shrimp and cook for a minute on high heat. Turn over the shrimp and cook for another minute. Reduce the heat and cook for 2 to 3 minutes, turning the shrimp occasionally for uniform cooking.

5 Sprinkle with the lemon juice and Thai basil. Serve hot.

fresh tomato soup with cilantro cream

Serves **4**   Preparation **10 minutes**   Cooking **15 minutes**

This is simple, hearty tomato soup made easy for the everyday cook. Serve hot with bread or rolls on a monsoon evening!

4 teaspoons oil
1 small yellow onion, diced
1 bay leaf
6 ripe medium tomatoes (about 2 lbs/1 kg), peeled and diced
2 tablespoons tomato paste
3 cups (750 ml) heavy cream
Salt, to taste
1 teaspoon freshly-ground black pepper
2 tablespoons chopped fresh coriander leaves (cilantro)

4 sprigs fresh coriander (cilantro), for garnish

Cilantro Cream
½ cup (125 ml) heavy cream
1 teaspoon finely-chopped fresh coriander leaves (cilantro)
Salt and freshly-ground pepper, to taste

1 To make the Cilantro Cream, whip the heavy cream, fresh coriander, salt and pepper until stiff peaks form. Refrigerate until ready to use.

2 Make the soup: Heat the oil in a large, heavy saucepan over medium heat. Add the yellow onion and bay leaf, and sauté until soft and translucent, about 4 minutes. Add the tomatoes and tomato paste, and bring to a boil. Reduce the heat to medium-low and simmer uncovered until the soup thickens, 15 to 20 minutes. Remove the bay leaf.

3 In a blender, purée the soup until smooth. Return to the pan and stir in the heavy cream, salt, pepper and chopped fresh coriander. Reheat gently.

4 Ladle into individual bowls and serve hot with 1 tablespoon of Cilantro Cream in each bowl. Garnish with cilantro sprigs.

yellow pear and cherry tomato salad with cumin

Serves 4   Preparation 15 minutes

I love the sweet and tart flavors of cherry and pear tomatoes. When mixed, they are appetizing on their own. Hence, I've kept the flavors in the dressing to a minimum here to enhance the tomatoes as much as possible. The ground cumin adds texture to this colorful dish.

2 tablespoons fresh lemon juice
2 tablespoons minced red onion
2 teaspoons honey
2 tablespoons extra-virgin olive oil
Salt, to taste
½ teaspoon red pepper flakes
2 teaspoons cumin seeds, toasted and coarsely ground (page 7)
2 cups (300 g) halved yellow pear tomatoes
1 cup (150 g) halved red cherry tomatoes

1 cup (150 g) halved orange cherry tomatoes
1 tablespoon chopped fresh basil

1 Combine the lemon juice, red onion, honey, olive oil, salt, red pepper flakes and ground cumin in a small bowl. Whisk until well blended.
2 Gently toss all the tomatoes together in a large salad bowl. Pour the dressing on top, add the chopped basil and gently toss to mix well. Serve immediately.

tropical fruit salad with chili lime vinaigrette

Serves 4   Preparation 15 minutes

I call for pineapple and mangoes in this recipe, but feel free to add other sweet fruits from the tropics, like papayas, kiwis and melons. The red onions, chili flakes and balsamic vinegar complement the sweetness of the fruit.

5 tablespoons white balsamic vinegar or white wine vinegar
3 tablespoons fresh lime juice
1½ teaspoons sugar
Salt, to taste
2 teaspoons red pepper flakes
½ cup (125 ml) extra-virgin olive oil
1 large, firm, ripe mango, peeled and cut into ½-in (1.25-cm) cubes
1 lb (500 g) fresh pineapple, peeled, cored and cut into ½-in (1.25-cm) cubes
1 red onion, thinly sliced
1 small red bell pepper, deseeded and thinly sliced
1 cup (40 g) fresh coriander leaves (cilantro), chopped

1 Whisk the vinegar, lime juice, sugar, salt and red pepper flakes together in a large bowl until the sugar is dissolved. Add the oil in a thin stream, whisking until emulsified.
2 Add the mango, pineapple, red onion, red bell pepper and coriander, and toss until coated. Serve chilled.

carrot and cucumber salad with spiced mustard dressing

Serves 2 **Preparation 10 minutes** **Cooking 5 minutes**

This is a summer salad that's very simple to make. I have used yogurt instead of mayonnaise to give it a lighter feeling. Tempering the spices results in a headier flavor. The freshness of this dish is further accentuated when it is served chilled—ideally as part of a summer lunch menu.

4 tablespoons plain yogurt
2 tablespoons sesame seeds, toasted and ground
2 teaspoons cumin seeds, toasted and ground
½ lb (250 g) cucumbers, peeled, deseeded and diced
½ lb (250 g) carrots, grated
Salt, to taste
2 teaspoons oil
½ teaspoon black mustard seeds
1 small, fresh green chili pepper, slit lengthwise and deseeded
¼ teaspoon ground turmeric

¼ teaspoon Asian chili powder or ground cayenne pepper
1 tablespoon fresh lemon juice
2 tablespoons minced fresh mint leaves, for garnish

1 Toast the cumin seeds in a heavy-bottomed skillet over medium heat, until aromatic. Grind the toasted cumin seeds with a mortar and pestle or coffee grinder.

2 Combine the yogurt, sesame seeds and cumin seeds in a small bowl. Mix well to make a smooth paste. Mix in the cucumbers, carrots and salt. Set aside.

3 Heat the oil in a small skillet over medium heat. Add the black mustard seeds and chili pepper, and cook for about a minute, stirring until aromatic.

4 Add the turmeric and Asian chili powder to the skillet, stir, and immediately pour the flavored oil over the cucumber mixture.

5 Add the lemon juice and toss gently. Place in the refrigerator to chill thoroughly.

6 Serve cold topped with the mint leaves.

chicken skewers with soy ginger glaze

Serves 4   Preparation 10 minutes   Cooking 10 minutes

With a palate for most things spicy and robust, Indians have tailored Chinese cuisine to suit their taste buds. This chicken recipe is my Indianized version of a popular Chinese-American dish. The flavors of the spices in the garam masala complement the sweetness of the honey and the soy, resulting in a perfect balance in flavor.

4 skinless, boneless chicken
    breasts cut into 1-in (2.5-cm)
    cubes
Twenty 12-in (30-cm) wooden
    skewers
Orange slices, for garnish

Soy Ginger Marinade
¼ cup (65 ml) soy sauce
½ cup (125 ml) fresh orange juice
Zest of 1 orange
4 teaspoons oil
2 tablespoons honey
1 tablespoon deseeded and
    minced green chili pepper
2 teaspoons garam masala
2-in (5-cm) piece peeled and
    minced fresh ginger
2 cloves garlic, crushed

1 Combine the ingredients for the Soy Ginger Marinade in a small microwave-safe bowl. Heat in the microwave on medium for 1 minute, and then stir.
2 Place diced chicken breasts in a shallow dish. Pour the marinade over top and turn the chicken in the marinade to evenly coat. Set aside to marinate for 25–30 minutes.
3 Soak the skewers in water for 30 minutes while the meat marinates.
4 Preheat a grill to medium-high heat. Remove the chicken from the marinade, but do not discard the marinade.
5 Place 5 to 6 chicken cubes on each skewer, leaving a ⅛-in (3-mm) space between the cubes, and place the skewers on a pan.
6 Pour the marinade into a small saucepan. Bring to a boil, and then simmer over medium heat until it reduces to half, about 5 minutes. Set aside for basting.
7 Lightly oil the grill. Cook the chicken skewers on the prepared grill for 6 to 8 minutes per side, or until the juices run clear. Baste frequently with the Soy Ginger Marinade reduction until the chicken turns golden brown. Serve with orange slices and Soy Ginger Marinade reduction.

pan-roasted spiced corn

Serves **4**   Preparation **10 minutes**   Cooking **5 minutes**

Zipping up frozen corn with Indian spices makes it a very simple yet tasty accompaniment for even a non-Indian menu. The tangy fresh coriander offsets the sweetness of the corn and red bell pepper. The baby greens add just the touch of color and visual appeal to this simple dish.

2 teaspoons cumin seeds
½ teaspoon fennel seeds
2 dried red chili peppers
1 lb (500 g) frozen corn, thawed
2 tablespoons corn oil
1 small onion, finely chopped
Salt, to taste
1 red bell pepper, deseeded and finely chopped
3 tablespoons finely-chopped fresh coriander leaves (cilantro)
Mixed baby greens (purchase bagged as "mixed greens" or "baby greens")

1 Toast the cumin seeds, fennel seeds and red chili peppers in a small non-stick skillet over medium heat, stirring and shaking the skillet until the spices are highly fragrant and a few shades darker, about 2 minutes. Transfer to a bowl, let cool and grind finely in a spice or coffee grinder.

2 Place the corn in a non-stick skillet over medium-high heat and stir until the water evaporates. Transfer to a bowl.

3 Heat the oil in the same non-stick skillet over medium-high heat. Cook the onion, stirring until golden, 3 to 5 minutes. Add the corn, ground spices and salt, and cook until the corn is golden brown, 2 to 3 minutes.

4 Add the red bell pepper and fresh coriander leaves, and cook about 2 minutes. Cool to room temperature and serve over mixed baby greens.

butternut squash soup with exotic spices

Serves **6**   Preparation **10 minutes**   Cooking **35 minutes**

This soup warms the soul! The smooth, sweet butternut squash, when married with exotic coconut milk, curry powder and star anise, makes this is the perfect recipe for a family dinner on a cold night.

2 tablespoons unsalted butter
1 large onion, thinly sliced
2 bay leaves
2 star anise pods
1 cinnamon stick
1 tablespoon curry powder
1-in (2.5-cm) piece peeled and minced fresh ginger
3 cloves garlic, minced
2 lbs (1 kg) butternut squash, peeled and diced
Salt, to taste
1 teaspoon freshly-ground black pepper
2 cups (500 ml) unsweetened coconut milk
4 cups (1 liter) unsalted vegetable stock or water

1 Melt the butter in a large saucepan over medium heat. Add the onion, bay leaves, star anise and cinnamon, and cook, stirring until the onions are tender, about 5 to 7 minutes. Add the curry powder, ginger and garlic, and cook for 2 minutes. Add the squash, season with salt and pepper, and sauté for 1 minute.

2 Stir in the coconut milk and stock. Bring to a boil and then reduce to a simmer. Cook, stirring occasionally, until the squash is tender, about 20 to 25 minutes. Remove the bay leaves, star anise and cinnamon stick.

3 Purée the soup in a blender or food processor, working in batches until smooth. Strain through a fine sieve and season with salt and pepper if needed. Serve hot.

crispy fried fish with chili mayo

Serves 6   Preparation **20 minutes**   Cooking **15 minutes**

This is one of my favorites. It's best washed down with a pint of beer or two! The addition of spices to the batter makes it really tasty. Combine the fish with chili pepper-flavored dipping sauce, and it's irresistible!

4 skinless tilapia fillets (1½ to 2 lbs/750 g to 1 kg), cut into strips
Juice of 2 lemons
¼ **tablespoon ground coriander**
Salt, to taste
1 cup (135 g) all-purpose flour
1½ cups (375 ml) water
4-in (10-cm) piece peeled and minced fresh ginger
3 cloves garlic, minced
1 teaspoon cumin seeds
2 tablespoons chopped fresh mint leaves
Canola oil, for deep-frying
Lemon wedges, for serving

Chili Mayo Dipping Sauce
2 tablespoons prepared sambal chili paste
1 tablespoon minced green onions (scallions)
2 cups (400 g) low-fat mayonnaise

1 To make the Chili Mayo Dipping Sauce, combine the mayonnaise, chili paste and green onions in a bowl and mix well until blended.

Refrigerate until ready to use.

2 Rinse the fish strips clean and pat dry with paper towels. Transfer the fillets to a bowl and pour the lemon juice over top. Sprinkle on the ground coriander and season with salt. Marinate for an hour in the refrigerator.

3 Remove the fish fillets from the marinade and place on paper towels to remove any excess marinade.

4 Combine the flour and water in a medium bowl to make a smooth paste of coating consistency. Add the ginger, garlic, cumin seeds and mint, and season with salt.

5 Heat the oil to 350°F (175°C) in a wok or a deep-frying pan over medium heat. Toss the fish fingers into the flour mixture, and fry until golden brown and crisp, about 6 minutes. Remove with a slotted spoon and drain on a paper towel. Transfer to a serving dish and serve hot with lemon wedges and the Chili Mayo Dipping Sauce.

poultry

 In India, a large segment of the population is vegetarian, and meat is generally not eaten on the same scale as in the West. Nonetheless, meat is popular, and chicken—as here in the West—is the most popular of all.

In fact, in inland regions where seafood isn't as readily available, lamb, goat and chicken form the basis of many popular dishes.

In addition, India has a diverse array of religions and cultures, some of which do not follow vegetarian diets. Muslims, for example—who are meat eaters—have influenced Indian cuisine in various parts of the country.

I pick and choose my chicken recipes quite carefully. For example, I think that *vindaloo* paste can overpower the flavor of chicken. While I may make chicken *vindaloo* to change things up from time to time, I prefer to pair bold spices with the stronger flavor of pork (the traditional meat for *vindaloo*) or even duck.

Turkey is almost never used in India—it simply isn't available. However, I've tried many of these recipes with turkey, and find that it often works just as well as chicken.

tandoori chicken tikka with lemon and sage

Serves 6   Preparation 15 minutes   Cooking 15 minutes

This dish—loosely inspired by chicken tikka masala, an all-time favorite Indian dish in the West—makes for a very simple, yet satisfying meal. The bright flavors of sage, lemon and garlic marry very well to give the chicken a unique flavor. Quick to make, you can either marinate whole chicken breasts or cube them, as described in the following recipe. If preparing this dish with whole chicken breasts, serve with Aromatic Butternut Squash (page 97); its slight sweetness complements the sharp flavor of the sage-lemon marinade. When cubed, I like to place the meat in a wrap, for a quick lunch to go!

5 lbs (2.25 kg) skinless, boneless chicken breasts cut into 1-in (2.5-cm) cubes
20 (12-in/30.5-cm) wooden skewers
Oil, for brushing broiler pan
6 lemon wedges, for garnish

Lemon Sage Marinade
1 teaspoon cumin seeds, toasted (page 7)
1 teaspoon coriander seeds, toasted (page 7)

2 cups (490 g) plain yogurt
4 cloves garlic, chopped
2 tablespoons peeled and chopped fresh ginger
3 tablespoons oil
2 tablespoons fresh lemon juice
1 teaspoon grated lemon zest
2 tablespoons chopped fresh sage
Salt, to taste
½ teaspoon turmeric
1 teaspoon garam masala
Freshly-ground black pepper, to taste

1 teaspoon Asian chili powder or ground cayenne pepper

1 Purée the ingredients for the Lemon Sage Marinade in a blender until smooth.
2 Place the chicken in a large bowl and pour the marinade over top. Turn the chicken pieces in the marinade to evenly coat. Cover and refrigerate for 4 to 6 hours.
3 Soak the skewers in water for 30 minutes. While the skewers are

soaking, bring the chicken to room temperature.
4 Preheat the broiler to high heat.
5 Brush a broiler pan lightly with oil. Place 5 chicken cubes on each skewer, leaving a ⅛-in (3-mm) space between the cubes, and place the skewers on the pan. Broil the chicken about 4 in (10 cm) from the heat, turning once, until browned in spots and just cooked through, 10 to 12 minutes. Serve hot, garnished with lemon wedges.

pan-roasted onion chicken

Serves 6   Preparation **10 minutes**   Cooking **15 minutes**

Very quick and easy to make, this chicken preparation can easily be the "most valuable player" on your weekday dinner table. You can substitute chicken breasts with a whole chicken, place it right on the table, and have family members carve their favorite pieces. Serve it with a side of Baby Beets and Carrots with Curry Leaves (page 94).

2 tablespoons oil
1 teaspoon cumin seeds
1 large onion, diced
1 teaspoon garam masala
2 lbs (1 kg) chicken, skinned and
  cut into 1-in (2.5-cm) pieces
10 fresh curry leaves
2-in (5-cm) cinnamon stick
2 cardamom pods
1 tablespoon ground coriander
1 teaspoon ground cumin
Salt, to taste
1 cup (125 g) thinly-sliced and
  crisply-fried onions, for garnish
  (page 6)

1 Heat the oil in a large non-stick saucepan over medium-high heat. Add the cumin seeds, diced onion and garam masala, and cook until the onion is brown, about 5 minutes.
2 Add the chicken, curry leaves, cinnamon, cardamom, coriander, cumin and salt. Increase the heat and pan-roast the ingredients until brown, about 5 minutes, turning constantly.
3 Reduce the heat to medium-low and simmer covered until the chicken is tender, about 5 to 7 minutes. Add water if needed. Serve hot, garnished with the fried onions.

lemon pepper chicken with fresh mint

Serves **6**   Preparation **10 minutes**   Cooking **15 minutes**

Readymade lemon pepper powder—found in most households and widely available—is a great tool to make a simple, quickly-made yet delicious chicken dish. Here I have used this very common condiment as the inspiration for a flavorful marinade, using fresh lemon juice and zest. The green chili pepper and turmeric give it a little zing. Serve it with simple dinner rolls or a portion of the Southern Indian Masala with Potatoes and Peas (page 101), if you want to get a little more elaborate.

6 (4-oz/125-g) chicken breasts, trimmed of excess fat
2 tablespoons oil
1 large onion, thinly sliced
1 cup (8 g) fresh mint leaves, for garnish
1 lemon, sliced, for garnish

Lemon Pepper Marinade
1 tablespoon minced ginger
1 tablespoon minced garlic
1 tablespoon oil
Salt, to taste

1 tablespoon coarsely-ground black pepper
3 tablespoons fresh lemon juice
1 tablespoon freshly-grated lemon zest
½ cup (4 g) finely-chopped fresh mint leaves
1 small fresh green chili pepper, deseeded and minced
1 teaspoon ground turmeric

1 Combine the ingredients for the Lemon Pepper Marinade in a medium bowl.

2 Add the chicken to the marinade and mix well to evenly coat. Cover and refrigerate for 2 to 3 hours.

3 Heat the 2 tablespoons of oil in a large non-stick skillet over medium-high heat. Add the onion and cook, stirring often until golden, about 5 minutes. Add the chicken and cook until brown, about 3 minutes on each side.

4 Reduce the heat and continue to cook, covered, until the chicken is cooked through yet tender, about 5 to 7 minutes. Serve hot, garnished with mint leaves and lemon slices.

stir-fried chicken with cumin and peppers

Serves **4**   Preparation **10 minutes**   Cooking **20 minutes**

When chicken is lightly dredged in flour and stir-fried with peppers and some basic seasoning, it tastes plenty good as-is. I have added some cumin, vinegar and yogurt for flavor, but also to add a nice consistency and a little body. Serve these chicken pieces with a cup of piping hot Butternut Squash Soup with Exotic Spices (page 34) or serve it on a plate with a portion of Saffron Rice with Toasted Almonds (page 73).

1 lb (500 g) skinless, boneless chicken thighs, cut into 1-in (2.5-cm) pieces

1 tablespoon peeled and minced fresh ginger

1 tablespoon minced garlic

1 tablespoon cumin seeds, toasted and ground (page 7)

2 tablespoons malt vinegar

1 teaspoon coarsely-ground black pepper

Salt, to taste

2 tablespoons oil

1 teaspoon cumin seeds

½ cup (125 g) plain yogurt, whisked until smooth

1 large onion, diced

1 large red bell pepper, deseeded and diced

1 Place the chicken in a large bowl. Add the ginger, garlic, toasted and ground cumin, vinegar, black pepper and salt. Mix the ingredients, making sure all the chicken pieces are well covered with the marinade. Cover with plastic wrap and marinate in the refrigerator for 4 to 6 hours.

2 Heat the oil in a medium non-stick skillet and add the cumin seeds; they should sizzle upon contact with the hot oil. Quickly add the chicken pieces with all of the marinade and cook, turning as needed, until lightly golden on all sides, about 5 minutes.

3 Add the yogurt, stirring constantly to prevent it from curdling, and then mix in the onion and bell pepper and cook until all the juices evaporate and the chicken is a rich golden color, fully cooked and tender, about 10 to 15 minutes.

baked marinated chicken

Serves 6   Preparation **10 minutes**   Cooking **25 minutes**

Try this recipe for basic baked chicken with the breasts or the whole bird. You can even substitute turkey for the chicken, if that's what you have on hand. In fact, it wouldn't be a bad idea to give an Indian makeover to your traditional Thanksgiving turkey, and surprise your family and friends!

2 lbs (1 kg) skinless, boneless chicken breasts or thighs, cut into 2-in (5-cm) pieces
3 tablespoons canola oil
1 large onion, finely chopped
2 small fresh green chili peppers, deseeded and minced
1 cup (245 g) plain yogurt, whisked until smooth
2 tablespoons chopped fresh mint leaves

Yogurt-Mint Marinade
1 tablespoon peeled and minced fresh ginger
1 tablespoon minced garlic
2 tablespoons dried mint leaves
1 cup (245 g) plain yogurt, whisked until smooth
2 teaspoons garam masala
Salt, to taste

1 Mix the ingredients for the Yogurt-Mint Marinade together in a large bowl.

2 Add the chicken and mix well, making sure all the chicken pieces are well coated with the marinade. Cover with plastic wrap and marinate in the refrigerator 4 to 6 hours.

3 Preheat the oven to 350°F (175°C).

4 Heat the oil in an ovenproof saucepan with a tight fitting lid over medium heat, and cook the onion, stirring often until brown, about 7 minutes. Add the green chili peppers and stir for 1 minute. Add the yogurt a little at a time, stirring constantly to prevent it from curdling. Cook until it comes to a boil.

5 Mix in the chicken, plus the marinade. Cook, stirring for about 5 minutes. Remove from the heat and cover with the lid.

6 Place the pan in the oven and bake until the chicken is cooked through and tender, about 20 minutes. Serve hot, garnished with the mint leaves.

duck vindaloo curry

Serves **4**   Preparation **10 minutes**   Cooking **20 minutes**

Vindaloo, an Indian dish originating from Goa, was a result of the influence of Portuguese culture and lifestyle from when Goa was one of Portugal's colonies. Pork is by far the most traditional meat used with this preparation. However, here I have made it with duck, which marries surprisingly well to Indian tastes, spices and flavors. And though duck isn't readily available in India, it has been gaining popularity in Indian restaurants in the West.

5 dried red chili peppers, crushed
1 teaspoon black peppercorns
1 teaspoon cumin seeds
1 teaspoon black mustard seeds
1 tablespoon peeled and minced fresh ginger
1 tablespoon minced garlic
½ teaspoon sugar
Salt, to taste
¼ cup (65 ml) white vinegar
2 lbs (1 kg) skinless, boneless duck breasts, cut into 1-in (2.5-cm) pieces
3 tablespoons oil
1 large onion, minced
¼ cup (65 ml) dry red wine

1 Blend the dried chili peppers, peppercorns, cumin, mustard, ginger, garlic, sugar, salt and vinegar into a paste in a blender.
2 Place the duck and the spice paste in a bowl; turn the duck pieces to evenly coat them with the paste. Cover and refrigerate for 4 to 6 hours.
3 Heat the oil in a wide, heavy skillet over medium heat. Add the onion and sauté until softened and lightly browned, about 5 minutes.
4 Add the duck pieces (reserve excess seasoning paste) and sauté until the duck is browned on all sides. Add the reserved paste and the wine.
5 Bring to a boil, then cover and lower the heat; simmer for 10 to 12 minutes until the duck is tender and cooked.

 # cardamom chicken

Serves **6**   Preparation **10 minutes**   Cooking **20 minutes**

The sweetness of cardamom and coconut milk give a very distinctive and appealing flavor to chicken. Add some commonly-available vegetables from the refrigerator, like carrots, potatoes, beans or even mushrooms, to create hearty stew. For a complete meal, serve it with a portion of hot basmati rice, or a flat Indian bread like Toasted Cumin Chapatis with Orange (page 72).

20 cardamom pods
3 lbs (1.5 kg) chicken, cut into 2-in (5-cm) pieces
1 tablespoon peeled and minced fresh ginger
1 tablespoon minced garlic
2 cups (490 g) plain yogurt, whisked smooth
2 teaspoons freshly-ground black pepper
2 teaspoons freshly-grated lemon zest
2 tablespoons clarified butter
2 cups (500 ml) coconut milk
6 small fresh green chili peppers, slit in half and deseeded
2 tablespoons chopped fresh coriander leaves (cilantro)
Salt, to taste
3 tablespoons fresh lemon juice

1 Pry open the cardamom pods and extract the seeds. Grind the seeds to a fine powder using a spice or coffee grinder; discard the husks.
2 Place the chicken, ground cardamom seeds, ginger, garlic, yogurt, black pepper and lemon zest in a large bowl. Mix well until the chicken pieces are well coated. Cover and marinate for 4 to 6 hours in the refrigerator.
3 Heat the clarified butter in a heavy-bottomed skillet over medium-high heat. Add the chicken and cook for about 5 minutes on both sides, until brown.
4 Add the coconut milk, bring to a boil, and then add the chili peppers and fresh coriander. Simmer until the chicken is cooked through, 10 to 12 minutes. Season with salt and stir in the lemon juice.

golden roast chicken with green chili and spices

Serves **6**   Preparation **15 minutes**   Cooking **1 hour**

The delicate flavors of the spices with the whole chicken make this a one-of-a-kind dish that is just right for a special occasion. Although it is somewhat labor intensive, the outcome and the visual appeal of this dish more than make up for the difficulty of its preparation. I used to make this for festive family gatherings, and sometimes wrapped the whole chicken in banana leaves. Serve this when you want to surprise and impress someone!

3 tablespoons fresh lemon juice
1 tablespoon salt
1 (4-lb/1.75-kg) whole chicken
1 tablespoon oil
2 large onions, coarsely chopped
1 tablespoon peeled and minced
   fresh ginger
1 tablespoon minced garlic
5 small fresh green chili peppers,
   deseeded and minced
3 tablespoons ground almonds
1 teaspoon paprika
1 teaspoon turmeric
2 teaspoons garam masala
3 cups (120 g) fresh coriander
   leaves (cilantro), chopped

1 Combine the lemon juice and salt in a small bowl, and thoroughly rub the mixture over the entire chicken.
2 Heat the oil in a heavy-bottomed skillet over medium heat, add the onions and cook until they start to brown. Add the ginger, garlic and green chili peppers, and cook for 2 minutes, or until soft. Add the almonds, paprika, turmeric and garam masala. Cook, stirring frequently, for an additional

minute. Remove from the heat and allow the onion mixture to cool completely.
3 Place the cooled mixture in a food processor along with the chopped fresh coriander, and grind to a smooth paste. Rub the paste thoroughly all over the chicken and inside the cavity. Tie the legs of the chicken together to keep them in place. Cover and refrigerate for 6 to 8 hours.
4 Preheat the oven to 350°F

(175°C). Place the chicken in a roasting pan and bake until the chicken is cooked and tender, 45 to 50 minutes. Make sure you turn the pan around halfway through baking, for even cooking.
5 Baste the chicken with some of the pan juices and return it to the oven for 10 minutes or until brown, with well-roasted skin. Place the chicken on a serving platter. Serve hot, and carve tableside.

grilled chicken with apple compote

Serves 4 Preparation **10 minutes** Cooking **20 hour**

This dish was inspired by the flavor of kokum, a fruit very common to the Indian west coast, which is used in various dishes to impart a naturally sour taste. When this note of sourness is combined with apple compote, it gives an addictive sweet and sour taste to the dish. A trip to an Indian grocery store or an online source is needed to get the kokum. Although there is not a real substitute for the flavor of kokum, I suggest replacing it with raisins if necessary. I often like to pair this dish with Yellow Pear and Cherry Tomato Salad with Cumin (page 31) when I'm in the mood for a simple, yet exotic entertainment menu.

2 tablespoons coriander seeds

2 teaspoons cumin seeds

1 teaspoon cardamom seeds extracted from the pods

1-in (2.5-cm) piece cinnamon stick

1 onion, coarsely chopped

1 tablespoon peeled and chopped fresh ginger

½ teaspoon ground cloves

1 teaspoon Asian chili powder or ground cayenne pepper

¼ cup (65 ml) oil

Juice of 1 lemon

Salt, to taste

4 boneless chicken breasts (about 1 lb/500 g total), trimmed of excess fat

Apple Compote

2 tablespoons butter

2 Granny Smith apples, peeled, cored and chopped

½ cup (125 ml) apple cider

1 teaspoon coriander seeds, toasted and ground

1 teaspoon cumin seeds, toasted and ground

2 tablespoons seeded and chopped kokum (or raisins)

1 Place a small, dry skillet over low heat and toast the coriander, cumin, cardamom and cinnamon until aromatic. Grind the toasted spices to a fine powder using a spice or coffee grinder.

2 Place the onion, ginger, ground cloves, Asian chili powder, oil, lemon juice and salt in a blender or food processor and process until smooth.

3 Combine the ground, toasted spices with the onion paste in a bowl and thoroughly mix.

4 Slather the spice paste all over the chicken, cover, and place in the refrigerator to marinate for 2 to 4 hours.

5 While the chicken is marinating, make the Apple Compote: Cook the butter in small saucepan over high heat until golden brown. Add the apples and cook, stirring until caramelized, about 5 minutes. Add the apple cider and cook until the liquid had evaporated, about 5 to 7 minutes. Mix in the coriander, cumin and kokum and cook for 1 minute. Set aside until ready to use.

6 Preheat the grill to medium heat. Grill the chicken pieces for 5 minutes on each side, or until the chicken is tender and cooked with the meat white in the center. Serve hot, topped with the compote.

Chapter Four

Meat

 To Westerners, India is thought of as being a largely vegetarian country, and yet this is not necessarily true. To a larger extent than in the West, religious beliefs, rather than personal preference, dictate what a person will eat. Meat dishes are eaten in almost all regions of India. Whereas meat-eating Hindus and Muslims like lamb and chicken, Christians prefer pork and beef.

Meat became popular within Indian society during the Mughal rule and later on during the British rule in India. Military invasions and India's trade routes have left a marked foreign influence on the type of meat that is eaten and styles in which it is prepared—*vindaloo* from the Portuguese, kebabs and pilafs (*pulaos*) from the Greeks and Persians are examples of such influences. The methods of cooking meat in the south produce different flavors and use local produce, such as coconut, tamarind and curry leaves. Dishes from the south are hotter and spicier than those from the north. More often than not, these curries involve long and slow simmering to extract the juices from the meat.

There are hundreds of ways to prepare meat in the Indian style. It is quite often minced to make various kinds of kebabs and *koftas*. It is also used in stews, mixed with lentils, and often just braised with spices and eaten with bread or rice. All the dishes in this chapter are treated as the main dish in a meal, with the side dishes—appetizers, vegetables and accompaniments—planned around it.

grilled lamb chops with curried couscous

Serves 4   Preparation 15 minutes   Cooking 20 minutes

I have used couscous in this dish because it is almost a staple ingredient in most home pantries. Additionally, it goes wonderfully with most Indian dishes and flavors. Couscous has its own set of health benefits as well: it's high in fiber and is a healthy alternative to rice or bread. Serve this main course combo with a vegetable dish of your choice or with my favorite pairing, Sweet and Sour Asparagus with Cashews (page 106).

1 cup (245 g) plain yogurt
1 tablespoon garam masala
Salt, to taste
1½ lbs (750 g) ½-in (1.25-cm)-thick
   lamb chops
1 teaspoon curry powder
¼ teaspoon ground turmeric
⅛ teaspoon ground cinnamon
1 teaspoon paprika
1½ cups (375 ml) water
2 tablespoons butter
1½ cups (300 g) couscous

1 Mix together the yogurt, garam masala and salt in a small bowl. Marinate the lamb chops with the yogurt mixture overnight or for at least 4 hours.

2 Toast the curry powder, turmeric, cinnamon and paprika in a small heavy saucepan over medium heat, stirring constantly until fragrant, about 1 minute. Add the water, salt to taste and the butter, and bring to a boil. Place the couscous in a heatproof bowl and pour in the boiling water mixture. Quickly cover with plastic wrap and let it stand for 5 to 10 minutes.

3 Preheat the grill or broiler to 375ºF (190ºC) or to high heat.

4 Scrape off the excess marinade and grill the lamb chops, turning over once, for about 3 to 5 minutes on each side for medium doneness and set aside.

5 Fluff the couscous with a fork and transfer it onto a serving platter. Place the lamb chops over the couscous and serve hot.

indian-style beef burgers

Makes four ⅓-lb (150-g) burgers or eight 3-oz (80-g) sliders   Preparation **10 minutes**   Cooking **10 minutes**

These delectable patties can be served as appetizers or even as burger patties in a bun. My friends' kids absolutely love these burgers when I serve them with Pomegranate Mint Chutney (page 21) home-style potato fritters and a Sparkling Ginger-Lime Cooler (page 116).

1½ lb (750 g) lean ground beef
1 onion, finely chopped
2 teaspoons minced ginger
2 teaspoons ground cumin
2 teaspoons ground coriander
½ teaspoon Asian chili powder or
    ground cayenne pepper
2 teaspoons salt
2 fresh green chili peppers,
    deseeded and minced
1 teaspoon fresh lemon juice
¼ cup (10 g) fresh coriander leaves
    (cilantro), chopped
¼ cup (2 g) fresh mint leaves,
    chopped
Oil, for brushing the burgers
4 hamburger buns or 8 slider buns

1 Place the meat in a bowl. Add the onion, ginger, cumin, coriander, Asian chili powder, salt, chili and lemon juice, and mix well with your hands, turning, mashing and kneading to blend the flavors and to get a smooth texture. Cover and refrigerate the mixture for at least an hour.
2 Mix in the fresh coriander and mint leaves. With wet hands, mold the mixture into 4 equal-size patties or, to create sliders, 8 equal-size patties. Refrigerate the patties at least for 1 hour.

3 To grill the patties: Preheat the grill to high. Lightly oil the grate with vegetable oil—pour oil onto a paper towel, then hold the towel with tongs to wipe the oil onto the grate. Place the patties on the grill directly over the heat. Cook about 2 to 3 minutes per side for medium doneness, brushing with oil to prevent sticking, turning once.

4 While the meat is cooking, prepare the rolls. Slice and toast the bread on the grill. Serve the patties sandwiched between the bun halves.

Tip Do not press down on the patties with a spatula during cooking—this only squeezes out the juices and dries out the meat.

roasted rack of lamb with a mint crust

Serves 4   Preparation **15 minutes**   Cooking **30 minutes**

Coating meat with a crust is actually a French technique. The final outcome makes for a great presentation, so it is one of those dishes that you should make when the occasion calls for something impressive! The crumbed crust used here has flavors of mint and mustard that go very well with lamb. Serve it with a vegetable side like Zucchini with Yellow Mung Lentils and Roasted Garlic (page 105).

2 racks of lamb, about 2 lbs (1 kg) each, trimmed of excess fat
2 tablespoons fresh lemon juice
1 tablespoon peeled and minced fresh ginger
1 tablespoon minced garlic
1 teaspoon garam masala
Salt, to taste
1 slice whole-wheat bread, lightly toasted
1 tablespoon chopped fresh coriander leaves (cilantro)
2 tablespoons ground dried mint leaves
1 teaspoon cumin seeds
2 tablespoons oil
1 tablespoon Dijon mustard
4 fresh mint sprigs, for garnish

1 Preheat the oven to 450ºF (230ºC).
2 In a large bowl, combine the lemon juice, ginger, garlic, garam masala and salt. Place the lamb racks in the bowl and mix well, making sure all of the pieces are well-coated with the marinade.
3 Place the bread in a blender or food processor and pulse until it forms coarse crumbs. Add the fresh coriander, dried mint and cumin, and pulse to blend.
4 Heat the oil in a large oven-proof skillet over medium-high heat. Add the lamb to the pan and cook, turning as needed, until browned on both sides, about 5 minutes. Remove the pan from the heat and brush the mustard over the rounded top and the front side of the racks. Gently pat the bread crumb mixture into the mustard.
5 Roast in a preheated oven until a thermometer inserted into the meat reads 140ºF (60ºC) for medium-rare, 20 to 25 minutes. Transfer to a platter and let it rest.
6 To serve, cut the lamb between the ribs into separate bone-in chops. Garnish with mint sprigs.

classic marinated lamb curry

Serves **6** Preparation **10 minutes** Cooking **25 minutes**

This is a classic recipe, with no global twists to it! I have used boneless lamb here, but for additional flavor, and if you are willing to get your hands dirty, use a bone-in cut of lamb shoulder or leg. Serve with Puffed Breads with Mint (page 80) or Saffron Rice with Toasted Almonds (page 73).

2 lbs (1 kg) boneless leg of lamb, cut into 1-in (2.5-cm) cubes
3 tablespoons oil
5 cardamom pods
3 bay leaves
1-in (2.5-cm) cinnamon stick
1 teaspoon cumin seeds
1 tablespoon ground coriander
4 fresh green chili peppers, deseeded and minced
1 tomato, chopped
2 cups (500) ml water
1 cup (245 g) plain yogurt
½ cup (20 g) fresh coriander leaves (cilantro), chopped

Curry Yogurt Marinade
3 onions, chopped
1 tablespoon Asian chili powder or ground cayenne pepper
1 tablespoon ground cumin
½ tablespoon ground turmeric
½ cup (125 g) plain yogurt
2 teaspoons garam masala
Salt, to taste

1 In a blender or a food processor, blend together the Curry Yogurt Marinade ingredients until smooth.
2 In a large bowl, mix together the marinade and lamb, making sure the pieces are well coated. Cover with plastic wrap and marinate in the refrigerator at least 4 hours.
3 Heat the oil in a large non-stick saucepan over medium-high heat. Add the cardamom pods, bay leaves, cinnamon, and cumin seeds. They should sizzle in the oil. Quickly add the ground coriander. Mix in the lamb with the marinade and sauté over high heat, stirring for 5 minutes. Reduce the heat to medium-low, cover and cook until the juices are mostly dry, 15 to 20 minutes.
4 Add the green chili peppers, tomato, water, and 1 cup (245 g) of yogurt and bring to a boil over high heat. Reduce the heat to medium-low, cover and simmer until lamb is tender and sauce is thick.
5 Serve hot garnished with the fresh coriander.

lamb chops with rosemary and lime

Serves 6 Preparation 15 minutes Cooking 15 minutes

These elegant chops are simple to make, can be prepared in advance, and are a hit with my friends! The flavors make a delicious and fragrant sauce. I usually serve these chops with a side of Mango and Roasted Red Pepper Chutney (page 23), and some stir-fried seasonal vegetables.

1 tablespoon black peppercorns
1 teaspoon whole cloves
7 cardamom pods
1 tablespoon ground coriander
1 teaspoon ground cumin
½ teaspoon ground cinnamon
¼ teaspoon fresh ground nutmeg
1 cup (230 g) sour cream
1 tablespoon minced ginger
1 tablespoon minced garlic
Salt, to taste
¼ cup (10 g) finely-chopped fresh
    rosemary
2 tablespoons fresh lime juice
2 tablespoons oil
2 lbs (1 kg) bone-in lamb chops,
    trimmed of excess fat
1 cup (250 ml) water
2 sprigs fresh rosemary, for garnish
Lime wedges, for garnish

1 Grind together the peppercorns, cloves and cardamom in a spice or coffee grinder.
2 Toast the ground spices, coriander, cumin, cinnamon and nutmeg in a small non-stick skillet over medium heat, constantly

stirring until the spices are fragrant, about 2 minutes.
3 Mix together the toasted spices, sour cream, ginger, garlic, salt, rosemary, lime juice and one tablespoon of the oil in a large bowl. Add the lamb chops to the mixture and mix well, making sure all the pieces are well coated with the marinade. Cover with plastic wrap and marinate in the refrigerator at least 4 to 6 hours.
4 Remove the lamb chops and reserve the marinade. Heat 1 tablespoon of oil in a large non-stick skillet over medium-high heat, cook the lamb chops turning once until golden brown, about 5 minutes on each side.
5 Mix the water and reserved marinade together and add it to the skillet. Cover and cook over medium heat until the chops are tender and the sauce is thick, about 10 to 15 minutes.
6 Serve hot, garnished with the rosemary sprigs and lime wedges.

honey roasted stuffed lamb

Serves **6**   Preparation **20 minutes**   Cooking **1 hour**

Not an everyday dish, a stuffed leg of lamb is something you would want to make for special occasions. I live to serve this lamb dish with a portion of rice, like Basmati Rice with Dry-Roasted Spices (page 77). Note: You will need to ask your butcher to make the leg of lamb boneless, as it isn't something you can't do at home.

For the stuffing, you may use any vegetable of your choice, not necessarily the spinach and mushroom that I have used here.

1 (3½-lb/1.5-kg) leg of lamb, trimmed of excess fat, de-boned, and butterflied
¼ cup (65 ml) malt vinegar
2 tablespoons oil
Salt, to taste
1 teaspoon chili powder
1 cup (230 g) sour cream
1 onion, minced
1 tablespoon minced garlic
2 tablespoons warmed honey, plus extra for drizzling
1 teaspoon clarified butter
1 tablespoon ground coriander
1 teaspoon ground cumin
½ teaspoon Asian chili powder or ground cayenne pepper

Spinach and Nut Stuffing
1 lb (500 g) fresh spinach, chopped
½ lb (250 g) button mushrooms, chopped
1 cup (140 g) almonds, chopped
¼ cup (25 g) dried cranberries
1 cup (40 g) fresh coriander leaves (cilantro), chopped
1 tablespoon garam masala

1 Mix together the ingredients for the Spinach and Nut Stuffing in a large bowl.
2 Make 2-in (5-cm)-long, deep cuts, each about 2 in (5 cm) apart, over the entire outside surface of the leg of lamb.
3 Mix together the malt vinegar, oil, salt and chili powder in a bowl, and rub well over both sides of the meat, making sure you work it into all the cut sections. Spread the spinach mixture on the entire inside surface. Then roll the lamb into a log. Tie the roll with kitchen twine crosswise and then lengthwise to secure it.
4 Mix together the sour cream, onion, garlic, honey, clarified butter, coriander, cumin and Asian chili powder and rub well over the outside surface of the meat.
5 Cover with plastic wrap and marinate in the refrigerator for 6 to 8 hours.
6 Preheat the oven to 400°F (200°C).
7 Transfer the lamb to an ovenproof dish, along with its marinade, and roast for 30 to 40 minutes.
8 Reduce the heat to 300°F (150°C) and cook until the lamb is golden brown and tender, about 15 to 20 minutes.
9 Remove the string from the roast, cut the lamb into 1-in (2.5-cm) slices and serve hot, drizzled with honey.

aromatic lamb with green peas and cumin

Serves 6 **Preparation 15 minutes** **Cooking 30 minutes**

This dish is so good that I often make extra portions to use the next day. Ground beef can be substituted for the lamb.

3 tablespoons oil
2 onions, chopped
1 teaspoon cumin seeds
2 tablespoons peeled and minced fresh ginger
4 cloves garlic, minced
4 fresh green chili peppers, deseeded and minced
2 bay leaves
1 lb (500 g) ground lamb
2 tablespoons tomato paste
½ teaspoon ground turmeric
1 teaspoon Asian chili powder or cayenne pepper
2 tablespoons ground coriander
2 tablespoons plain yogurt
Salt, to taste
1 teaspoon freshly-ground black pepper
½ cup (125 ml) water
1 cup (150 g) frozen peas, thawed
½ teaspoon garam masala
2 tablespoons ground cumin
5 tablespoons chopped fresh coriander leaves (cilantro)

1 Heat the oil in a large saucepan over medium heat. Add the onions, cumin, ginger, garlic, green chili peppers and bay leaves and fry for 3 to 4 minutes, until golden brown. Add the ground lamb and fry for 15 minutes, stirring occasionally to prevent the meat from sticking.

2 Add the tomato paste, stir, and lower the heat to a simmer.

3 Add the turmeric, chili powder and ground coriander, and stir for 1 minute. Add the yogurt, salt and pepper, and continue frying for 5 minutes. Add the water and peas, and simmer until the lamb is cooked and tender, about 10 minutes.

4 Stir in the garam masala, cumin and coriander before serving.

spicy goan beef curry

Serves 6 **Preparation 15 minutes** **Cooking 50 minutes**

If the Indian state of Goa was to be branded by one of its most popular dishes, it would be without any contest, Vindaloo! This recipe is influenced by Goan Vindaloo, but lighter in taste and texture. Serve it with basmati rice for a sumptuous meal!

7 dried red chili peppers
¼ cup (65 ml) malt vinegar
3 cloves garlic
4-in (10-cm) piece peeled and chopped fresh ginger
1 large onion, chopped
1 tablespoon cumin seeds
3 teaspoons coriander seeds
2 teaspoons black mustard seeds
1 teaspoon ground cinnamon
½ tablespoon soy sauce
½ teaspoon ground turmeric
Salt, to taste
2 lbs (1 kg) beef, cut into 1-in (2.5-cm) pieces
3 tablespoons oil
5 fresh curry leaves
3 tablespoons tomato paste
3 cups (750 ml) water
1 tablespoon chopped fresh coriander leaves (cilantro)

1 Combine the red chili peppers and vinegar in a small bowl and set aside to soak for about 2 hours.

2 Grind together the soaked dried chili peppers with the vinegar, garlic, ginger and onion in a food processor until a fine paste has formed. Mix in the cumin, coriander, black mustard seeds, cinnamon, soy sauce, turmeric and salt. Blend again to make a smooth paste.

3 Combine the spice paste and the beef in a large bowl; mix well, making sure all the pieces are well coated with the marinade. Cover with plastic wrap and marinate in the refrigerator for at least 4 to 6 hours.

4 Heat the oil in a large non-stick saucepan over medium-high heat. Add the curry leaves and the beef with all the marinade. Increase the heat to high and cook, stirring until the pieces are well-browned, about 5 to 7 minutes. Add the tomato paste and water, reduce the heat to medium and cook until the beef is tender, about 30 to 40 minutes.

5 Serve hot, garnished with the fresh coriander.

east indian chili con carne

Serves 6   Preparation 20 minutes   Cooking 1 hour

This is an Indian version of the American Chili con Carne, using some Indian spices for that special unique taste. You can use ground veal, chicken, or turkey for this dish, but be mindful of the cooking time, since they cook in much less time than beef. I have practically made this my signature dish whenever I have a big party at home. It's wholesome, yet very economical when you have a large number of people to entertain. Serve it with a portion of rice—Basmati Rice with Dry-Roasted Spices (page 77) is a nice choice—or some bread-rolls for a simple yet satisfying meal.

2 tablespoons oil
1 teaspoon cumin seeds
4 dried red chili peppers
1 teaspoon black mustard seeds
1 large onion, finely chopped
½ cup (50 g) grated coconut
1 tablespoon peeled and minced
    fresh ginger
1 clove garlic, minced
2 tablespoons minced fresh curry
    leaves
1 tablespoon ground coriander
¼ teaspoon ground turmeric

1 teaspoon garam masala
Salt, to taste
1 lb (500 g) lean ground beef
One 8-oz (250-g) can kidney beans,
    rinsed and drained
1 tomato, chopped
1 cup (250 ml) water
1 cup (250 ml) coconut milk
½ cup (20 g) fresh coriander leaves
    (cilantro), chopped

1 Heat the oil in a large saucepan over medium-high heat, add the cumin seeds, red chili peppers and mustard seeds. They should splatter upon contact with the hot oil.

2 Add the onion and sauté, stirring constantly until softened, about 2 minutes. Mix in the coconut, ginger, garlic, curry leaves, coriander, turmeric, garam masala and salt. Stir until the mixture is golden, about 5 minutes.

3 Add the ground meat. Cook, stirring until the meat is slightly brown, about 10 minutes.

4 Add the beans, tomato and water, and bring to a boil over high heat. Reduce the heat to medium-low and simmer until the sauce is thick, about 10 minutes. Add the coconut milk and half of the fresh coriander and simmer for another 5 minutes. Serve hot, garnished with the remainder of the fresh coriander.

kashmiri meatballs

Serves **4**   Preparation **10 minutes**   Cooking **35 minutes**

Paprikash is a traditional Hungarian food that is very rich on the palette—a comfort dish to many. Authentic preparations feature onions sautéd in lard. I have used some aromatic spices to give it an Indian twist, including paprika, which is easily available at the grocery store. I use sour cream instead of the heavy cream to cut down on the richness of the dish. You could use meatballs that are available in the frozen aisle at your grocer's or, if you have the time, you can make the meatballs from scratch as described here. Serve this with Indian breads like the Fresh-Baked Rosemary Naan (page 75).

2 tablespoons oil
1-in (2.5-cm) cinnamon stick
1 teaspoon cumin seeds
1 large onion, chopped
1 tablespoon paprika
½ teaspoon salt
1 large tomato, diced
1 cup (230 g) sour cream
½ cup (125 ml) water, as needed
1 tablespoon chopped fresh
   coriander leaves (cilantro)

Spiced Meatballs
2 lbs (1 kg) lean ground lamb
4-in (10-cm) piece peeled and
   chopped fresh ginger
1 tablespoon ground fennel seeds
1 teaspoon garam masala
1 teaspoon ground cumin
½ teaspoon ground cardamom
1 tablespoon salt

1 To make the Spiced Meatballs, add the lamb, ginger, fennel, garam masala, cumin, cardamom and salt in a food processor. Grind the mixture until smooth.
2 Divide and shape the meat mixture into 2-oz (50-g) portions. Refrigerate until ready to use.
3 Heat the oil in a large saucepan over medium-high heat. Add the cinnamon stick, cumin seeds and onion, and cook until the onion is golden brown, about 10 minutes. Add the paprika and the salt and fry for 30 seconds. Stir in the tomato, remove from the heat, and slowly stir in the sour cream.
4 Carefully add the chilled meatballs and bring to a boil. Simmer, uncovered, for 30 to 40 minutes, over very low heat until the meatballs are tender and the sauce is thick. Add up to ½ cup (125 ml) of water, if necessary, during cooking to maintain a thick, sauce-like consistency. Serve garnished with the fresh coriander.

chipotle pork chops

Serves 4   Preparation 15 minutes   Cooking 30 minutes

I love experimenting with the various kinds of Mexican chili peppers. For this dish I substitute Mexican chili peppers for the traditional Indian choices, which gives this tikka an absolutely unique sweet and smoky flavor. As a variation to the method given below, you could skewer individual pieces of meat and grill them outdoors. If I'm serving this dish indoors, I like to offer a side of a Cannellini Dal Fry (page 86) and Spinach and Thyme Roti Flatbreads (page 76).

4 boneless pork loin chops, 1½ in
   thick
3 tablespoons oil
1 large red onion, minced
1 clove garlic, minced
1-in (2.5-cm) piece peeled and
   minced fresh ginger
¼ cup (65 ml) water
1 dried chipotle chili, chopped
½ cup (20 g) fresh coriander leaves
   (cilantro), chopped
1 teaspoon garam masala

Chipotle Chili Marinade
1 onion, minced
3 cloves garlic, minced
2 tablespoons peeled and minced
   fresh ginger
½ tablespoon ground cumin
1 teaspoon ground coriander
4 teaspoons chipotle chili powder
Salt, to taste
1 cup (245 g) plain yogurt, whisked
   until smooth

1 To make the Chipotle Chili Marinade, mix the onion, garlic, ginger, cumin, coriander, chipotle chili powder, salt and yogurt in a large bowl. Season the chops with the marinade on both sides. Cover and marinate in the refrigerator for 2–4 hours.

2 Heat the oil in a heavy-bottomed skillet, large enough to fit the meat in a single layer. Add the onion, garlic and ginger, and stir for about 4 minutes. Increase the heat to medium high and add the pork chops with the marinade. Cook the meat for 2–3 minutes on each side, and then reduce the heat to medium. Add the water and chili, and let the meat and juices simmer for 10–15 minutes. Cook until the pork is tender.

3 Serve hot, garnished with the fresh coriander and sprinkled with garam masala.

Chapter five

seafood

 For Indians, except those who are vegetarian, seafood or fish can figure into any and every meal. Though it has long been enjoyed along India's abundant coastline and inland from freshwater lakes and rivers, fish and seafood have become increasingly popular of late for their versatility and healthfulness.

Along India's miles and miles of coastline are many small fishing villages, home to the population of fisherman who make their living from the sea—an important occupation in India. Inland, India is dotted with several freshwater lakes, ponds, and rivers, which yield a sweeter-fleshed fish than those captured from salty seawater.

Fish can be cooked in many different styles and in every conceivable way: poached or steamed, deep-fried or pan-fried, baked, grilled, broiled, or smoked. Fish is truly good for you; low in calories and high in protein. Easy to digest and naturally tender, fish cooks quickly no matter what method you use.

The most common method of cooking and serving fish and seafood in Indian homes is as a curry, and so it is usually accompanied by rice. Other popular techniques are pan-frying and deep-frying. When fish or seafood is pan-fried, it is coated with spices; when deep-fried, it is coated with a batter or a crust. Baking and grilling is not done very often in homes in India. In restaurants, in addition to the traditional home-style cooking methods, fish may be grilled or baked in a *tandoor* oven to create tandoori-style fish dishes.

The majority of the seafood that is available in your local grocery takes well to Indian flavors. Most Indian recipes can be made with varieties that are easy to find in the West, such as sea bass, halibut, salmon, snapper, haddock, cod or even swordfish.

grilled sea bass with coriander chipotle ketchup

Serves **6** Preparation **10 minutes** Cooking **10 minutes**

This one's a summer favorite. The coconut milk provides a lovely mild sweetness along with the spices that have been used as marinade. The canned chipotle is usually found as "chipotles in adobo sauce" in the market. Serve with a fresh summer salad.

2 tablespoons coconut milk
1 tablespoon peeled and minced fresh ginger
1 tablespoon minced garlic
1 teaspoon red pepper flakes
3 tablespoons malt vinegar
2 teaspoons ground cumin
¼ teaspoon ground clove
½ teaspoon ground cinnamon
1 teaspoon ground paprika
Salt, to taste
1 tablespoon oil, plus more for brushing grill grate
2 lbs (1 kg) sea bass fillets (or other firm-fleshed fish such as tilapia or salmon), about 1 in (2.5 cm) thick, cut into 2-in (5-cm) pieces
Lemon wedges, for garnish

Coriander Chipotle Ketchup
2 large tomatoes, diced
1 small onion, chopped
½ tablespoon minced garlic
2 tablespoons tomato paste
1 tablespoon red wine vinegar
3 oz (85 g) canned chipotle chili peppers, minced
2 teaspoons ground cumin
Salt, to taste
1 tablespoon chopped fresh coriander leaves (cilantro)

1 Mix together all the ingredients in a large bowl, except the fish and lemon wedges.
2 Add the fish and gently mix, making sure all the pieces are well-coated. Cover with plastic wrap and marinate in the refrigerator for at least 4 hours.
3 While the fish is marinating, make the Coriander Chipotle Ketchup. Combine the tomatoes, onions, garlic, tomato paste, vinegar, chipotle chili, cumin and salt in a small saucepan over medium-high heat, and bring it to a boil. Reduce the heat to medium and simmer, stirring until the liquid is reduced and thick, about 5 to 7 minutes. Cool before serving.
4 Preheat the grill to medium-high (375°F/190°C) or a grill pan over medium-high heat. Brush the grill or grill pan with oil to prevent the fish from sticking to the grill.
5 Place the marinated pieces on the grill and cook, turning once or twice, until the fish is opaque and just flaky inside, and lightly charred on the outside, 5 to 7 minutes. Serve hot with lemon wedges and Coriander Chipotle Ketchup.

roasted red snapper with fresh green chili cilantro pesto

Serves 6 (makes about 1 cup/300 g pesto)   Preparation 15 minutes   Cooking 45 minutes

You can substitute any other whole firm-fleshed fresh fish. The pesto can be made ahead, making this a good dish for entertaining. This recipe will feed four when served with rice and a vegetable dish.

1 whole red snapper, about 2 to 2½ lbs (1 to 1.25 kg), cleaned and scaled
½ cup (125 ml) fresh lime juice
½ teaspoon grated lime zest
2 tablespoons oil
Salt, to taste
1 cup (180 g) Green Chili Cilantro Pesto, plus extra for serving (recipe follows)

Green Chili Cilantro Pesto
2 cups (80 g) chopped fresh coriander leaves (cilantro)
6 fresh green chili peppers, deseeded and minced
1 tablespoon minced garlic
2 teaspoons peeled and minced fresh ginger
2 tablespoons water
1 cup (100 g) fresh or frozen grated coconut
1 teaspoon cumin seeds, toasted and coarsely ground
3 tablespoons fresh lime juice
1 teaspoon sugar
Salt, to taste

1 To make the Green Chili Cilantro Pesto, place the fresh coriander, chili peppers, garlic, ginger and water in a food processor and process to a paste. Add the coconut and process to incorporate. Transfer to a bowl. Add the coarsely ground cumin.
2 Stir in the lime juice, sugar and salt. Use immediately or refrigerate, covered, until ready to serve. The pesto can be refrigerated for about 4 days in a well-sealed container.
3 Preheat the oven to 400°F (200°C).
4 Score the skin of the fish in a diamond pattern.
5 Combine the lime juice, lime zest, 1 tablespoon of the oil and salt in a shallow pan.
6 Place the fish in the pan and rub it all over with the lime mixture.
7 Rub 1 cup of the pesto mixture into the slits and put the remainder in the fish's cavity. Lay the fish on the sheet of aluminum foil, pour the remaining 1 tablespoon oil over the fish and spread it evenly over the top of the fish.
8 Lightly coat a shallow baking

dish with cooking spray. Wrap the aluminum foil fairly tightly around the fish: Use another piece of foil if necessary to ensure that the package is well sealed. Place it in the prepared baking dish.
9 Bake for about 30 minutes; the exact cooking time will depend on the size of the fish. To test, peel back the foil a little and press on the flesh at the thickest part of the fish. It should yield a little and feel

soft. You can also unwrap more of the fish and test with a fork: if it flakes, it's cooked.
10 Serve the fish warm on a platter, with extra pesto alongside as a condiment. Serve by lifting sections of the top fillet off the bone; when the first side is finished, flip the fish over to serve the second fillet. Drizzle all excess pan juices on top of the fish.

pan-braised fish with lemon and rosemary

Serves 6 Preparation 10 minutes Cooking 10 minutes

Lemon and rosemary infused in butter smell and taste wonderful! It's that heavenly combination that inspires this dish. Using any firm fish available in the market, this is a very simple-to-make yet flavorful main course. Serve it alongside a portion of rice. My friends like when I serve it with Stir-Fried Mushroom and Vegetable Pilaf (page 79), but you can always serve it with a simple side of buttered basmati rice.

6 tilapia fillets, about 6 oz (175 g)

Salt, to taste

1 teaspoon Asian chili powder or ground cayenne pepper

Juice of 1 lemon

3 teaspoons oil

2 red onions, thinly sliced

4 cloves garlic, minced

2 tablespoons peeled and minced fresh ginger

2 fresh green chili peppers, minced

1½ cups (375 ml) vegetable stock

3 tablespoons malt vinegar

2 teaspoons grated lemon zest

1 sprig fresh rosemary

1 Season the tilapia fish fillets on both sides with salt, chili powder, and lemon juice.

2 In a large, non-stick skillet, heat 2 teaspoons of the oil over medium-high heat. Add the fish to the pan and sear on both sides until lightly browned, about 2 minutes on each side. Transfer to a plate and keep warm.

3 Add the remaining 1 teaspoon of oil to the pan and add the onions, garlic, ginger and green chili peppers and sauté for 1 minute.

4 Stir in stock, vinegar, lemon zest, and rosemary. Return the tilapia to the pan. Cover and simmer until the fish is opaque throughout, about 3 to 4 minutes.

5 Transfer the tilapia fillets to a serving platter. Spoon some sauce over each fillet and serve.

goan crab cakes

Serves 4   Preparation **15 minutes**   Cooking **10 minutes**

These delicious crab cakes can be served as an appetizer or a main course. The beauty of crab cakes is that they can be made in advance, kept frozen, and fried when required. If you're serving these cakes as part of a meal, serve it with Spicy Red Lentils (page 87), Southern Indian Masala with Potatoes and Peas (page 101) or plain basmati rice.

½ cup (100 g) uncooked basmati rice, rinsed and drained
1 cup (250 ml) water
Salt, to taste
1 teaspoon plus 1 tablespoon oil
1 small red onion, chopped
1 clove garlic, minced
1 tablespoon peeled and minced fresh ginger
½ tablespoon fresh green chili pepper, deseeded and minced
7 oz (200 g) fresh or frozen lump crabmeat
1 tablespoon fish sauce
½ teaspoon chili sauce
2 tablespoons chopped fresh coriander leaves (cilantro)
1 egg, lightly beaten
3 tablespoons semolina
Fresh coriander (cilantro) sprigs, for garnish

1 In a saucepan, combine the rice, water and salt. Bring to a boil, and then reduce the heat to low and cover. Simmer until the water is absorbed and the rice is tender, 15 to 20 minutes. Set aside.

2 Heat the 1 teaspoon of oil in a small skillet over medium heat. Add the onion and sauté until translucent, about 5 minutes. Stir in the minced garlic, ginger, and green chili pepper and sauté until softened, about 1 minute.

3 In a large bowl, combine the crabmeat, onion mixture, fish sauce, chili sauce, fresh coriander and cooked rice. Toss gently with a fork to combine. Stir in the egg and mix until well blended.

4 Sprinkle the semolina on a sheet of baking paper. Divide the crab mixture into 4 portions and form each into a 3½-in (9-cm) patty. Dredge each patty in the semolina.

5 In a large skillet, heat the 1 tablespoon of oil over medium-high heat. Add the patties to the pan and fry, turning once, and until golden brown on both sides, about 5 minutes on each side. Top with fresh coriander sprigs, and serve hot.

coriander crusted salmon with cilantro cucumber chutney

Serves **6**   Preparation **10 minutes**   Cooking **10 minutes**

I love the flavor of salmon, and often try to keep the supporting flavors very delicate to showcase the taste of the fish. This is a simple yet flavor-packed salmon dish. I grind whole toasted spices to crust the salmon. I like to serve this dish with a fresh tropical salad. Choose between the chutney mentioned in this recipe or try plating this with a side of the Carrot and Cucumber Salad with Spiced Mustard Dressing (page 32).

6 salmon fillets, each 5 oz (140 g) and about 1 in (2.5 cm) thick
Salt and freshly-ground black pepper to taste
3 tablespoons coriander seeds, toasted and coarsely ground
2 teaspoons garam masala
2 teaspoons oil
Lime wedges, for garnish

Cilantro Cucumber Chutney
1 cucumber, peeled, halved lengthwise, seeded and thinly sliced
1½ cups (210 g) cherry tomatoes, quartered
½ red bell pepper, deseeded and cut into 1 in (2.5 cm) thick slices
3 tablespoons chopped red onion
2 tablespoons chopped fresh coriander leaves (cilantro)
2 tablespoons fresh lime juice
1 teaspoon oil
2 teaspoons honey
1 teaspoon red pepper flakes
Salt, to taste

1 Make the Cilantro Cucumber Chutney by combining the cucumber, tomatoes, bell pepper, onion and fresh coriander in a bowl. Toss gently to mix.
2 Whisk together the lime juice, oil, honey, red pepper flakes and salt in a small bowl. Pour the lime juice mixture over the cucumber mixture and toss gently; set the chutney aside.
3 Prepare the salmon: Season the salmon fillets on both sides with salt and pepper. Crust the salmon fillets on one side with the coriander seeds and garam masala.
4 Heat the 2 teaspoons of oil in a large, non-stick skillet over medium-high heat. Add the fish to the pan crust side down, cook, turning once, until opaque throughout when tested with the tip of the knife, 4 to 5 minutes on each side.
5 Transfer the salmon fillets to individual serving plates and top each with some of the Cilantro Cucumber Chutney. Serve hot, garnished with lime wedges.

fragrant lobster curry

Serves **4**   Preparation **15 minutes**   Cooking **10 minutes**

This simple dish boasts fragrant ginger, chili and cilantro. It's fantastic served over Basmati Rice with Dry-Roasted Spices (page 77).

4 fresh medium-size lobsters, about 2 lbs (1 kg)
1 cup (250 ml) fish stock or water
¾ cup (185 ml) oil
1½ teaspoons black mustard seeds
2 garlic cloves, minced
1-in (2.5-cm) piece peeled and minced fresh ginger
1 large red onion, sliced
½ teaspoon Asian chili powder or ground cayenne pepper
1 teaspoon turmeric
2 teaspoons salt, more as needed
1 large tomato (about ½ lb/250 g), chopped
One 14-oz (400-ml) can unsweetened coconut milk
4 tablespoons chopped fresh coriander leaves (cilantro), for garnish

Note: Live lobsters should be chilled and prepared on the day of purchase.

1 To prepare lobsters, plunge the tip of a large sharp knife straight down behind the eyes. Separate tails from bodies. Cut off fanned tail shells. Pull out the alimentary canal. Slice tails through lengthwise (first snip through the under-shell with scissors). Clean and wash the lobsters thoroughly.

2 Bring the fish stock to a boil in a large saucepan, add lobster bodies and tails and boil for 4 to 5 minutes. Remove from the pot and set aside. Strain and retain the stock for the sauce. Pull the meat from the shells, cut it into small chunks and set aside.

3 Heat the oil in a large skillet over medium heat. Add the mustard seeds and sauté until they begin to pop. Add the garlic and ginger and stir for 5 seconds. Quickly add the onion and sauté until a light golden color, about 2 to 3 minutes. Add the Asian chili powder, turmeric and salt and cook for 30 seconds to allow the flavors to intensify.

4 Add the chopped tomato and cook, stirring for 2 to 3 minutes. Add the coconut milk and the remaining stock; bring to a boil, stirring occasionally. Add the lobster meat and cover, reduce the heat to low, and simmer for 3 to 4 minutes. Add more salt, to taste. Garnish with the fresh coriander leaves and serve hot.

 # cumin crusted sea scallops

Serves **4**   Preparation **10 minutes**   Cooking **5 minutes**

This is yet another very easy-to-make main course. Its unique flavor comes from the use of aromatic spices like cumin and star anise. Serve it with a Rosemary Lemon Rice (page 74) for a simple yet satisfying weekday meal.

3 tablespoons Asian chili powder or ground cayenne pepper
3 tablespoons toasted cumin seeds, ground
1 teaspoon salt
1 teaspoon freshly-ground black pepper
12 sea scallops, rinsed and patted dry
¼ cup (65 ml) olive oil
1 teaspoon black mustard seeds
2 cardamom pods
1 star anise pod

1 Combine the chili powder, cumin, salt and pepper in a medium shallow bowl. Dredge one side of each scallop in the spice mixture.

2 Heat the oil in a large non-stick saucepan over high heat. Add the mustard seeds, cardamom, and star anise, cook for about 30 seconds. Place the scallops in the heated pan, spice side down, and cook for 20 seconds. Reduce the heat to low, turn the scallops and cook for 2 to 3 minutes more.

3 Remove from the pan and arrange the scallops on a serving platter. Drizzle the spice oil drippings from the pan over the scallops and serve.

crispy southern indian fried fish

Serves 6   Preparation **10 minutes**   Cooking **5 minutes**

Fried fish is a nearly universal favorite food all over India—especially during the monsoon season. Often when stuck indoors on a rainy day, a bunch of my cousins and I would serve ourselves our favorite drinks and accompany them with pieces of fried fish. Even today, when planning a dinner for a rainy evening at home with close friends, I would definitely include a dish of fried fish on the menu!

2 lbs (1 kg) firm fish fillets, such as
  sole, halibut or pomfret, cut into
  3-in (7.5-cm) pieces
Salt, to taste
1 tablespoon fresh lemon juice
⅓ cup (50 g) rice flour or all-purpose flour
2 teaspoons Asian chili powder or
  ground cayenne pepper
1 teaspoon ground fennel
2 cups (500 ml) oil, for deep-frying
4 to 6 lemon wedges, for garnish

1 Place the fish pieces on a large platter. Sprinkle with salt and the lemon juice and marinate about 30 minutes in the refrigerator.

2 Mix together the rice flour, chili powder, and fennel in a flat pan or plate.

3 With a paper towel, dry each piece of fish, and then dredge it in the rice flour mixture.

4 Heat the oil in a large non-stick skillet over medium-high heat until it reaches 350°F (175°C) on a deep-fry thermometer.

5 Deep-fry the fish until golden brown and crispy. About 4 to 5 minutes.

6 Transfer to a tray lined with paper towels to drain. Serve hot, garnished with lemon wedges.

tiger prawn curry with lemongrass

Serves 6   Preparation 10 minutes   Cooking 10 minutes

Influenced by Thai ingredients, the lemongrass and coconut infusion makes this dish very fragrant and delicious. Be careful not to overcook the prawns; otherwise, they will become rubbery, and would spoil the dish. Serve this with a portion of plain basmati rice to make it a delicious meal.

1 large red onion, sliced
½ cup (125 ml) oil
2 cloves garlic, minced
1-in (2.5-cm) piece peeled and minced fresh ginger
3 fresh green chili peppers, deseeded and minced
1 stalk lemongrass, trimmed, with tough outer leaves removed, and chopped
2 tablespoons ground coriander
1 teaspoon ground cumin
1 teaspoon ground turmeric
Salt to taste
1 teaspoon freshly-ground black pepper
¼ teaspoon ground cinnamon
¼ teaspoon ground cloves
One 14-oz (400-ml) can coconut milk
2 lbs (1 kg) jumbo tiger prawns or jumbo shrimp (about 24 total), shelled and deveined

1 Add the onion and oil to a large saucepan. Cover and cook on medium-high heat, stirring occasionally until slightly brown. Add the remaining ingredients except the coconut milk and prawns or shrimp and cook over medium heat, stirring occasionally, about 5 to 7 minutes.
2 Pour in the coconut milk and bring the sauce to a boil, stirring. Add the prawns and simmer uncovered, stirring occasionally until just cooked through, 3 to 5 minutes. Serve hot.

curried malabar squid

Serves **6**   Preparation **10 minutes**   Cooking **15 minutes**

For most people, squid are an acquired taste. While growing up in India, for some unknown reason, I hadn't discovered its existence during my foodie-expeditions, even though it was available and I have always seen it in the local fish market. But, since the years I've lived in the West, I have tried, tested, and prepared these squid in more ways than one, with my friends and guests as guinea pigs, and they always ask for more! This particular preparation is from the southern states of India, but fortunately you will find most of these ingredients at your local grocery store. Be careful not to overcook the squid as it will turn rubbery.

1 teaspoon cumin seeds
1 teaspoon coriander seeds
1 teaspoon fennel seeds
2 teaspoons Asian chili powder or ground cayenne pepper
1 teaspoon ground turmeric
2 lbs (1 kg) fresh squid, cleaned and cut into 1-in (2.5-cm) rings
2 teaspoons soy sauce
1 tablespoon chopped green onions (scallions)

2 tablespoons oil
2 onions, thinly sliced
10 fresh curry leaves
4 cloves garlic, crushed
2 tablespoons minced ginger
½ cup (125 ml) coconut milk
3 tablespoons fresh lime juice
Salt, to taste

1 Dry toast the cumin, coriander and fennel seeds in a small skillet over low heat until aromatic, about 2 to 3 minutes. Using a spice or coffee grinder, grind the toasted seeds to a fine powder with the chili powder and turmeric.

2 In large bowl, toss the squid with the spice mixture, soy sauce, and green onions.

3 Heat the oil in a heavy-bottomed skillet over medium-high heat. Add the onions and sauté until lightly browned. Add the curry leaves, garlic, ginger, and the marinated squid. Sauté, stirring constantly for one minute.

4 Add the coconut milk. Bring to a boil. Simmer for 2 to 3 minutes, or until cooked and tender. Stir in the lime juice, season with salt, and serve.

konkan chili shrimps

Serves 6   Preparation **10 minutes**   Cooking **10 minutes**

An Indo-Chinese recipe, this preparation of prawns is very popular in the streets of some major metropolitan cities in India. I often make these for my Indian friends, which never fails to make them nostalgic for the things they miss back home. You can make this dish really quickly and serve it for a weekday dinner along with a portion of Rosemary Lemon Rice (page 74).

1 tablespoon canola or corn oil

1 tablespoon peeled and chopped fresh ginger

3 cloves garlic, chopped

2 shallots, chopped

10 fresh curry leaves

36 fresh medium shrimps, peeled and deveined

1 tablespoon soy sauce

2 tablespoons fresh lemon juice

2 tablespoons chopped dried red chili peppers

2 tablespoons minced fresh coriander leaves (cilantro)

¼ cup (60 g) low-fat plain yogurt, whisked until smooth

Salt, to taste

2 tablespoon chopped green onions (scallions), for garnish

1 Heat the oil in a wok or very large sauté pan over very high heat until smoking hot. Add the ginger, garlic, shallots, and curry leaves and sauté for 1 minute.

2 Add the shrimps and cook just until they start to turn pink, 2 to 3 minutes.

3 Add the soy sauce, lemon juice, dried chili peppers, and fresh coriander and cook, stirring often, 2 minutes longer. Add the yogurt and cook until the shrimps are just cooked through. Season with salt and serve warm garnished with green onions.

breads and rice

Bread, particularly flatbread, is a fundamental part of the dinner table in India. Most of these unleavened breads are easy enough to be made fresh daily at every meal. With the exception of a few breads, like *naan* (see Fresh-Baked Rosemary Naan, page 75), they are made entirely or mostly with whole-grain flours and are great tasting and rich in nutrients. They are usually rolled on a flat surface with a rolling pin and cooked on a hot surface—the exception being *poori* (see Puffed Breads with Mint, page 80), which is deep-fried in hot oil.

The variety of flatbreads found in Indian cuisine is amazing. In this chapter I have included a sampling of some of the most popular and familiar Indian breads, but there are many more available to the adventurous bread enthusiast. The recipes and methods of cooking breads differ widely from one part of India to another, with each region having its own specialties that vary in form, composition, and of course flavor.

Rice, used almost always to complement main dishes, is a staple in most households in India. Rice is also combined with lentils and vegetables, and is not just used as a side dish; there are also a large number of recipes where rice is an important ingredient in its own right. *Biryani* (Saffron Rice and Chicken Casserole, page 81) is probably the most famous of these rice dishes in the West.

The best variety of rice to use in savory dishes is *basmati*, which translates as "the fragrant one." If you can't get your hands on authentic Indian rice, it's okay to experiment with various kinds that are found at the supermarket.

toasted cumin chapatis with orange

Serves **4**   Preparation **10 minutes, plus 30 minutes (dough rest)**   Cooking **10 minutes**

This is by far the simplest Indian bread to make, and is the most common form of bread; it's made every day in northern Indian homes from rural villages to modern Indian cities. It is made with atta, which is wheat flour. The beauty of this dough is that is can be made up to a week in advance and refrigerated, and kept for future use. Use it as a wrap with any filling of your choice for your lunch box the next day.

2 cups (270 g) whole wheat flour
½ teaspoon salt
2 teaspoons cumin seeds, toasted and coarsely ground
Zest of 1 orange
1 cup (250 ml) water, or more as needed
½ cup (100 g) clarified butter

1 Toast the cumin in a medium pan over medium heat, stirring until fragrant, about 2 minutes. Remove from the pan and let cool.

2 Sift the whole wheat flour and salt into a bowl. Add the cumin and orange zest, and then mix well. Make a well in the center. Add the water, and mix until the flour is completely incorporated to form soft dough. Turn the dough onto a floured work surface and knead for 5 minutes. Place in an oiled bowl, cover, and let rest for 30 minutes. (This resting period makes the chapatis soft and fluffier.)

3 Heat a griddle pan or large cast-iron skillet over medium heat. Divide the dough into 8 equal portions. Working with one portion at a time and keeping the rest covered, on a lightly floured surface, roll out each portion to a 6-in (15-cm) circle. Remove the excess surface flour prior to cooking.

4 Place each rolled bread on the griddle, leave it to brown, about 7 to 10 seconds. Turn it over to brown on the other side, about 12 to 15 seconds. Turn over and smear the hot bread with clarified butter. Serve hot.

saffron rice with toasted almonds

Serves 4   Preparation 15 minutes   Cooking 15 minutes

Although saffron is an expensive ingredient, it is very often used in traditional Indian cooking because of the wonderful flavor and color that it imparts to the dish. For this preparation, you can use some or all of the spices mentioned in the recipe. Serve this with Spice Stuffed Okra (page 100) and Cannellini Dal Fry (page 86).

½ teaspoon saffron threads
¼ cup (65 ml) warm milk
2 tablespoons oil
1 tablespoon peeled and minced fresh ginger
1 teaspoon cumin seeds
6 cardamom pods
½ teaspoon black peppercorns
1 cup (200 g) uncooked basmati rice, washed in 3 to 4 changes of water
2 cups (500 ml) water
1 teaspoon salt
¼ teaspoon garam masala
½ cup (50 g) sliced almonds, toasted

1 Soak the saffron in the milk for about 15 minutes. Heat the oil in a large non-stick saucepan over medium-high heat and sauté the ginger, cumin, cardamom and black peppercorns, about 1 minute. Add the rice and water, season it with salt, and bring to a boil over high heat. Reduce the heat to lowest setting, cover the pan (partially at first, until the foam subsides, then snugly), and cook until the rice is almost done, 8 to 10 minutes.

2 Uncover the pan, sprinkle the saffron milk over the rice, then cover the pan and cook another 5 minutes to blend the flavors. Do not stir the rice while it's cooking.

3 Serve hot, sprinkled with garam masala and toasted almonds.

rosemary lemon rice

Serves **6**   Preparation **15 minutes**   Cooking **15 minutes**

Lemon rice is a very popular everyday dish in southern India. Rosemary, however, isn't a very popular ingredient in India, and is largely unavailable. I have combined these two flavors as they marry fantastically with one another. Serve it with a portion of Cardamom Chicken (page 43) and Green Cabbage with Lentils (page 99).

1½ cups (300 g) uncooked long-grain white rice
2 sprigs fresh rosemary
2 teaspoons lemon zest
3 cups (750 ml) water
¼ teaspoon ground turmeric
Salt, to taste
2 tablespoons fresh lemon juice
2 tablespoons oil
1½ teaspoons black mustard seeds
1 teaspoon red chili flakes
2 (1-in/2.5-cm) cinnamon sticks
2 whole cloves

1 Put the rice, rosemary, lemon zest, water, turmeric and salt in a large saucepan and bring to a boil over medium-high heat. Reduce the heat to low, cover the pan, and simmer until all the water has been absorbed and the rice is tender, 12 to15 minutes. Mix in the lemon juice, cover, and keep warm.
2 Heat the oil in a small non-stick saucepan over medium-high heat. Add the mustard seeds, red chili flakes, cinnamon, and cloves. Cook, stirring, about 1 minute. Add it to the rice, mix in and serve hot.

potato and dill stuffed parathas

Makes **14**   Preparation **15 minutes**, plus **30 minutes** (dough rest)   Cooking **20 minutes**

Stuffed parathas are a comfort food for many Indians. When I make them, I usually eat them with some plain yogurt and Wasabi and Green Chili Chutney (page 20). You could easily use leftover Mustard Potatoes with Dill (page 96) as the stuffing for this paratha.

4 cups (540 g) all-purpose flour
1 teaspoon salt
2 tablespoons oil
½ cup (100 g) clarified butter

Potato and Dill Filling
2 tablespoons oil
¼ teaspoon black mustard seeds
1 small onion, chopped
1 fresh green chili pepper, deseeded and minced
2 cups (35 g) fresh dill, chopped
½ lb (250 g) potatoes, boiled, peeled, and mashed
Salt, to taste

1 Sift the flour and salt into a large bowl and make a well in the center. Add the 2 tablespoons of oil and about 1¼ cups (300 ml) of water and mix into a soft, pliable dough.
2 Turn out onto a floured surface and knead for 5 minutes. Place in an oiled bowl, cover, and allow to rest for 30 minutes.
3 Make the Potato and Dill Filling by heating the oil in a saucepan over medium heat. Add the mustard seeds and, as soon as they begin to pop, add the onion and fry for 1 minute. Stir in the green chili pepper and dill, and cook for another 2 minutes. Add the potatoes and cook over low heat for 5 minutes. Season with salt and cool.
4 Divide the dough into 14 portions and roll each into a 6-in (15-cm) circle. Spread 1 tablespoon of the filling evenly over one-half of each circle of dough and fold into a semicircle. Rub oil on half of the surface and fold over into quarters. Roll out until doubled in size. Cover the parathas with a cloth.
5 Heat an oiled griddle or large cast-iron skillet over medium heat. Remove the excess flour from the parathas and cook each one for 2 to 3 minutes, then turn over and cook until slightly brown, lightly brushing with clarified butter. Serve warm.

fresh-baked rosemary naan

Serves 4   Preparation 10 minutes, plus 20 minutes (dough rest)   Cooking 10 minutes

Although naan is a rather popular form of an Indian bread, it is not usually made at home for the simple reason that the oven in which it is baked—the tandoor oven—is not found in most households. This recipe, however, gives you the closest texture and taste possible using a regular household oven. If you really wish to get closer to the flavor of naan baked in an Indian tandoor, acquire a baking stone or a pizza stone, heat it up, and use that to prepare this bread. Naan can be enjoyed with almost all gravy dishes, however, I prefer to have it with the Chipotle Pork Chops (page 57) or Baked Marinated Chicken (page 42) and any raita.

4 cups (540 g) all-purpose flour
1 package (about 0.6 oz/18 g) dry
    active yeast
2 teaspoons nigella seeds
½ teaspoon baking powder
½ teaspoon salt
3 tablespoons chopped fresh
    rosemary
1 egg, whisked
2 tablespoons clarified butter
¾ cup (180 g) plain yogurt
1¼ cups (300 ml) milk, warmed (to
    about 110°F/43°C)

1 Sift the flour into a large bowl and make a well in the center. Add the yeast, nigella seeds, baking powder, salt and rosemary. In another bowl, mix the egg, clarified butter, and yogurt. Pour 1 cup (250 ml) of warmed milk into the flour and mix to form a soft dough. If the dough seems dry add the

remaining ¼ cup (65 ml) of milk.
2 Turn onto a floured work surface and knead for 5 minutes, or until smooth and elastic. Put in an oiled bowl, cover, and leave in a warm place to double in size, about 2 to 3 hours.
3 Preheat the oven to 400ºF (200°C).
4 Punch down the dough, knead it briefly and divide into 10 portions. Roll out the dough into 6 or 7-in (15 to 18-cm) circles. Arrange the rolled breads on a greased baking sheet. Bake on the top shelf for 7 minutes, and then turn the naan over and bake for another 5 minutes. Serve hot.

spinach and thyme roti flatbreads

Makes 15   Preparation 10 minutes, plus 30 minutes (dough rest)   Cooking 10 minutes

This is basically made with the same dough as the Potato and Dill Stuffed Parathas (page 74); I have simply used different ingredients to flavor it. Feel free to use a variety of dry spices or greens to make the chapati more interesting to the eye and the palate.

4 cups (200 g) spinach leaves, cooked and chopped

4 cups (500 g) all-purpose flour

1 teaspoon salt

½ cup (32 g) fresh thyme leaves, chopped

1 teaspoon oil, plus more for oiling griddle

1 cup (250 ml) water

1 cup (100 g) melted clarified butter

1 Squeeze the extra water out of the spinach. Sift the flour and salt into a bowl and make a well in the center. Add the spinach, thyme, oil and water to the well and mix to form a soft, pliable dough.

2 Turn out the dough onto a floured surface and knead for 5 minutes. Place in an oiled bowl, cover, and allow to rest for 30 minutes.

3 Divide the dough into 15 balls. On a lightly-floured surface, evenly roll out each portion to a very thin 6-in (15-cm) circle.

4 Heat a griddle or large cast-iron skillet over medium-high heat, oil it lightly, and cook the roti one at a time. Cook for 2 to 3 minutes on each side. The roti will fluff and brown around the edges. Brush lightly with clarified butter and serve warm.

basmati rice with dry-roasted spices

Serves 4   Preparation 15 minutes   Cooking 15 minutes

This is a very simple way to turn an everyday rice dish into something exciting and flavorful. The flavor of toasted spices in the rice marries very well with any vegetable or meat dish, and can be used as your standard rice for any Indian fare. You can even make this dish with just one of the spices, like the cumin or the peppercorns, instead of using the entire array.

1½ teaspoons cumin seeds
1 teaspoon whole cloves
½ teaspoon black peppercorns
5 to 7 green cardamom pods
1½ cups (300 g) uncooked basmati rice, washed in 3 to 4 changes of water, and drained
1 tablespoon oil or clarified butter
2¾ cups (600 ml) water
1 teaspoon salt
1 tablespoon finely-chopped fresh mint leaves

1 Place the cumin seeds, cloves, black peppercorns, and the cardamom in a medium saucepan and toast, stirring and shaking the pan, over medium-high heat until highly fragrant, about 1 minute.

2 Add the drained rice and oil or clarified butter and continue to toast another 1 to 3 minutes, stirring gently, without breaking the grains of the rice.

3 Add the water and salt, and bring to a boil over high heat. Reduce the heat to the lowest setting, cover the pan, and cook until the rice is done, 10 to 15 minutes. Do not stir the rice while it cooks. Remove from the heat and let the rice rest for 5 minutes. Transfer to a serving platter, garnish with mint, and serve.

mint pilaf with potatoes and cumin

Serves **6** Preparation **15 minutes** Cooking **15 minutes**

One of my personal favorites, I end up making this pilaf for my family and friends very often. Although it's one of my comfort foods, I make it when entertaining as well. When served with Beet and Pineapple Raita (page 23), it makes for a hearty meal.

3 teaspoons cumin seeds, toasted
  and coarsely crushed
2 tablespoons oil
1 small onion, thinly sliced
1 small potato, peeled and cut into
  ½-in (1.25-cm) dice
1½ tablespoons peeled and
  minced ginger
2 tablespoons minced fresh mint
  leaves
1 fresh green chili pepper,
  deseeded and minced
1¼ cups (250 g) uncooked basmati
  rice, rinsed and drained
2¼ cups (550 ml) water
1 teaspoon salt

1 Toast the cumin in a medium pan over medium heat, stirring until fragrant, about 2 minutes. Remove from the pan and let cool. Crush the seeds and set aside.

2 Heat the oil in a large saucepan over medium-high heat and sauté the onion until brown, about 5 to 7 minutes. Add the potato, ginger, half of the mint and the green chili and cook, stirring, about 2 minutes.

3 Add the drained rice and sauté for 3 minutes. Add the water and salt, and bring to a boil over high heat. Reduce the heat to the lowest setting, cover the pan and cook until the rice is done, 10 to 15 minutes. Do not stir the rice while it cooks. Remove from the heat and let the rice rest for about 5 minutes.

4 Transfer to a serving platter, sprinkle the toasted cumin and the remaining mint on top, and serve.

spicy eggplant rice with mint

Serves 6   Preparation 15 minutes   Cooking 15 minutes

A childhood friend often used to make this dish for me—Vaangi Baath, as it is known in India. I have added a twist—mint—for extra flavor. You can use Asian baby eggplants or the regular ones for this recipe. Serve it with a Potato Raita with Chives and Cumin (page 19).

1 cup (75 g) dried unsweetened coconut

8 dried red chili peppers, broken

1½ teaspoons coriander seeds

1 teaspoon cumin seeds

2 teaspoons sesame seeds

½ teaspoon seeds extracted from whole green cardamom pods

½ teaspoon black peppercorns

¼ teaspoon ground turmeric

¼ teaspoon ground cloves

¼ teaspoon ground cinnamon

2 tablespoons oil

1 tablespoon black mustard seeds

1 tablespoon minced fresh curry leaves

1 lb (500 g) eggplant, cut into 1-in (2.5-cm) pieces

Salt, to taste

1 tablespoon tomato paste

4 cups (800 g) basmati rice, cooked (follow recipe for Basmati Rice with Dry-Roasted Spices, page 77, omitting the spices)

2 tablespoons chopped fresh mint leaves

1 Toast the coconut, red chili peppers, coriander, cumin, sesame seeds, cardamom and black peppercorns in a medium pan over medium heat, stirring until fragrant, about 2 minutes. Remove the spices from the pan and let cool. Grind the spices to a fine powder in a spice or coffee grinder. Place in small bowl and mix in the turmeric, cloves, and cinnamon.

2 Heat the oil in a large saucepan over medium-high heat and add the mustard seeds; they should splutter upon contact. Quickly add the curry leaves, eggplant, salt, and half the ground spice mix. Cover the pan and cook over medium-high heat the first 2 to 3 minutes, then reduce the heat to medium and cook until the eggplant is quite soft, about 10 minutes.

3 Add the tomato paste and cook about 2 minutes. Gently mix in the cooked rice, mint and the remaining ground spice mix. Cover and cook over low heat, 5 to 7 minutes, to blend the flavors. Serve hot.

stir-fried mushroom and vegetable pilaf

Serves 6   Preparation 15 minutes   Cooking 15 minutes

Leafy vegetables aren't a common addition to rice-based dishes in India—red chard, in fact, is unavailable there—but the food value from these greens is a good reason to include them. They also provide a great contrasting color. If you can't get red chard, try rainbow chard or even spinach or kale. Serve this alongside Grilled Sea Bass with Coriander Chipotle Ketchup (page 60) or Roasted Red Snapper with Fresh Green Chili Cilantro Pesto (page 61) and a green salad.

2 cups (500 ml) water

1½ cups (300 g) uncooked basmati rice, rinsed and drained

Salt, to taste

1 teaspoon cumin seeds, toasted

3 tablespoons oil

1 lb (500 g) white button mushrooms, cleaned and quartered

1 lb (500 g) red chard, trimmed, washed and finely chopped

1 large clove garlic, minced

2 fresh green chili peppers, deseeded and minced

1 teaspoon salt

1 tablespoon fresh chopped coriander leaves (cilantro)

1 Bring the water to a boil in a medium saucepan, and then add the rice, salt and cumin seeds. Bring to a boil again, then reduce the heat to low, cover, and simmer until the water is absorbed and the rice is tender, about 10 to 15 minutes. Transfer to a large bowl and keep warm.

2 Add 1 tablespoon of the oil to a large saucepan over medium-high heat. Add the mushrooms to the hot oil and cook until they are golden and release their juices, 5 to 7 minutes. Reserve in a bowl.

3 Add the remaining 2 tablespoons of oil and the red chard to the same pan and cook, stirring, over medium-high heat until the chard is wilted, about 3 minutes. Add the garlic, green chili peppers and salt, reduce the heat to medium, cover the pan, and cook until the leaves are soft, 7 to 10 minutes. Mix in the mushrooms.

4 Spoon the mushroom and red chard mixture on top of the rice and serve hot, garnished with fresh coriander leaves.

puffed breads with mint

Serves 4   Preparation 10 minutes, plus 30 minutes (dough rest)   Cooking 15 minutes

For best health, deep-fried foods should not be eaten very often, but these Indian breads are great for special occasions. Mint adds to the color and flavor of this bread, and makes for a great presentation. I would serve this with a portion of Street-Style Spicy Black Chickpea Masala (page 90), Hot and Sour Chickpeas (page 88) or Mustard Potatoes with Dill (page 96).

1 cup (135 g) whole-wheat flour
½ cup (65 g) all-purpose flour
¼ teaspoon cumin seeds, coarsely ground
¼ teaspoon salt
10 fresh mint leaves, minced
3 tablespoons oil
⅓ to ½ cup (80 to 125 ml) water
Oil, for deep-frying

1 Blend all the dry ingredients and the fresh mint leaves together in a food processor, or mix by hand in a bowl. Add the oil and, when blended, add ⅓ cup (80 ml) of the water and mix until a dough is formed, adding more water if needed.

2 Turn the dough onto a floured work surface and knead for 5 minutes. Place in an oiled bowl, cover, and let rest for 30 minutes.

3 Divide the dough into 8 equal portions. Apply oil to both sides of the dough balls and flatten each into discs about 3 to 4 in (7.5 to 10 cm) in diameter with a rolling pin.

4 Fill a medium saucepan ⅓ with oil for deep-frying and heat oil on high. Deep-fry the bread, turning once to ensure that it puffs up. Drain on paper towels. Serve immediately.

saffron rice and chicken casserole

Serves 6   Preparation **45 minutes**   Cooking **1 hour**

Biryani, as this is known in India, is a labor-intensive preparation. Hence, reserve this for special occasions. This is a one-pot meal, but adding a simple raita to it will make it even more nutritious. Leftovers of this dish are even more flavorful, so make an extra portion!

2 lbs (1 kg) chicken, skinned and cut into serving pieces
4 cups (1 liter) water
1½ cups (300 g) uncooked basmati rice, rinsed and drained
2 tablespoons oil or clarified butter
4 whole mace
6 cardamom pods
1 (1-in/2.5-cm) cinnamon stick
2 bay leaves
2 teaspoons cumin seeds
2 tablespoons chopped fresh mint leaves
2 tablespoons chopped fresh coriander leaves (cilantro)
1 teaspoon saffron threads, soaked 5–10 minutes in ¼ cup (65 ml) warm milk
1½ cups (150 g) sliced onions, crisply fried (page 6)
2 tablespoons cashew nuts, toasted

Biryani Marinade
5 large cloves garlic
1 (3-in/7.5-cm) piece peeled fresh ginger

1 tablespoon chopped fresh mint leaves
2 fresh green chili peppers, stemmed
1 cup (10 g) fresh coriander leaves (cilantro), coarsely chopped
2 tablespoons fresh lime juice
2 cups (490 g) nonfat plain yogurt, whisked until smooth
1 tablespoon garam masala
Salt, to taste

1 Make the Biryani Marinade by blending the garlic, ginger, mint, green chili peppers, coriander and lime juice in a food processor or a blender to make a smooth purée. Transfer to a bowl and mix in the yogurt, garam masala, and salt. Add the chicken and mix well, making sure all the pieces are well coated with the marinade. Cover and marinate for at least 8 hours or overnight in the refrigerator.
2 Preheat the oven to 350ºF (175ºC).
3 In a large non-stick saucepan, bring the water to a boil over high heat and add the rice. Return the

water to a boil, then reduce the heat to medium-low and cook, uncovered, until the rice is half cooked, about 7 to10 minutes. Drain the rice and discard the water.
4 Heat the oil over medium-high heat in a large non-stick, oven-safe saucepan with a tight-fitting lid.
5 Add the mace, cardamom pods, cinnamon, bay leaves and cumin seeds, stirring constantly until fragrant, about 1 minute.
6 Add the marinated chicken with all the marinade and sauté, stirring frequently, until lightly brown,

about 5 to 10 minutes. Remove from the heat.
7 Sprinkle the mint and coriander on top of the chicken, then cover everything well with the partially cooked rice. Top the rice with the saffron milk, seal the pan well with aluminum foil, and place the lid tightly over the foil.
8 Bake for about 30 minutes. Remove from the oven, fluff the top of the rice lightly with a fork, arrange the fried onions and toasted cashew nuts on top and serve hot.

Chapter seven

beans

 Dals, though souplike in consistency, are much thicker than a typical Western soup. They are made with dried beans, usually lentils, and are an important source of much needed protein in a vegetarian diet, or to supplement minimal amounts of meat. *Dals* are eaten along with the meal, and often treated like an additional vegetable. They can often serve as a simple accompaniment to rice or a *roti*.

Dals are probably the most common and significant dishes in India—no Indian meal is complete without them. They are eaten in all parts of India in various forms ranging from spicy to mild, and mostly vegetarian. In certain parts of India, meats are also incorporated into *dals* to make them a complete meal.

Most *dal* recipes are quite simple to prepare. The standard preparation of *dal* begins with boiling a single variety or mix of *dal*, or beans, in water with some turmeric and salt to taste. When tender, the *dal* is combined with tempered spices.

Dals are easily the most convenient dish to prepare as part of a weekday Indian meal! Included in this chapter are some nontraditional legumes, such as cannellini and petit pois, that are easily available in your local supermarket. If your local grocery has an Indian section, you will easily find the rest of the dry beans in that aisle. If not, your last and most successful resort would be the local Indian store!

chickpeas with spinach and fingerling potatoes

Serves **6**   Preparation **15 minutes**   Cooking **35 minutes**

Commonly known as garbanzo beans in the U.S., the chickpea is also a staple in the Indian kitchen. Like most legumes, chickpeas are very high in dietary fiber and protein. The addition of spinach, which is extremely rich in anti-oxidants and vitamins, and fingerling potatoes, rich in starch and carbohydrates, makes this dish a wholesome and complete meal for vegetarians.

1 lb (500 g) fingerling potatoes
Salt
3 tablespoons oil
2 teaspoons cumin seeds
1 large onion, chopped
¼ teaspoon ground turmeric
½ tablespoon crushed red chili
  flakes
1 tablespoon peeled and minced
  fresh ginger
1 tablespoon minced garlic
1 lb (500 g) fresh spinach, trimmed,
  rinsed and chopped
2 cups (320 g) dried chickpeas,
  washed, soaked overnight and
  drained, or one 16-oz (400-g)
  canned chickpeas, drained and
  rinsed well
1½ cups (375 ml) water
½ cup (20 g) fresh coriander leaves
  (cilantro), finely chopped
1 tablespoon ground coriander
2 small tomatoes, cut into 6
  wedges each

1 Boil the potatoes in lightly salted water until soft, about 20 minutes. Let them cool, and then cut into 1-in (2.5-cm) pieces.

2 Heat the oil In a large saucepan over medium-high heat and add the cumin seeds; they should sizzle upon contact with the hot oil. Quickly add the onion and turmeric, reduce the heat to medium and cook, stirring, until slightly brown, about 3 minutes.

3 Add the crushed red chili flakes, ginger and garlic and stir for 1 minute. Then add the spinach and cook, stirring until wilted, about 3 minutes.

4 Add the potatoes, chickpeas, water and fresh coriander, and bring to a boil over high heat. Cover the pan, reduce the heat to medium, and cook until the chickpeas are well blended and fragrant, about 5 minutes. Mix in the ground coriander and cook for another 3 minutes. Serve hot garnished with tomato wedges.

black-eyed peas with mushrooms

Serves 6   Preparation **15 minutes, plus 8 hours (dried pea soak time)**   Cooking **1 hour**

Black-eyed peas are rich in protein and carbohydrates; a great source of energy. A traditional ingredient in the southern U.S., the lobia bean, as it is known in India, is often used as a staple legume in vegetarian households. The mushrooms add to the wholesomeness of this dish. Dried peas soaked overnight taste best, but canned peas work as well. This dish is a favorite vegetarian offering for its full and robust flavor.

1 cup (180 g) dried black-eyed peas, soaked and drained, or 2 (15-oz/425-g) cans black-eyed peas, drained

4 cups (1 liter) water

½ teaspoon salt, plus more, to taste

½ cup (125 ml) oil

1 teaspoon cumin seeds

1-in (2.5-cm) cinnamon stick

1 cup (150 g) chopped red onion

4 cloves garlic, minced

½ lb (250 g) button mushrooms, cleaned and sliced

1 lb (500 g) ripe tomatoes, blanched and chopped

2 teaspoons ground coriander

1 teaspoon ground cumin

½ teaspoon ground turmeric

¼ teaspoon paprika

2 tablespoons chopped fresh coriander leaves (cilantro)

1 If using dried black-eyed peas, combine the peas, water and the ½ teaspoon of salt in a large saucepan. Bring to a boil, cover, and simmer until the peas are tender, about 45 minutes.

2 Drain the peas, rinse with cold water, drain again and transfer to a large bowl to cool.

3 Heat the oil in a heavy bottomed skillet or saucepan to medium high heat. Add the cumin seeds and cinnamon stick, and let them sizzle for 10 seconds. Add the onion and garlic and stir over medium heat until soft and starting to brown, about 5 minutes. Add the mushrooms and fry for 2 to 3 minutes. Add the tomatoes, ground coriander, cumin, turmeric and paprika. Cover and cook over low heat for 10 minutes.

4 Add the cooked or canned black-eyed peas to the tomato and mushroom mixture and season with salt, to taste. Stir in the fresh coriander leaves and simmer, uncovered, for 10 minutes.

cannellini dal fry

Serves 6   Preparation **15 minutes, plus 8 hours (dried bean soak time)**   Cooking **1 hour**

Cannellini beans are very popular in Mediterranean cooking. Here, I use them with Indian spices, which adds a unique dimension to the beans. These beans are low in fat, high in fiber, and contain more iron than red meat! Use canned beans if the dried variety is not available.

1 cup (180 g) dried cannellini beans, washed, soaked overnight and drained, or two 15-oz (425-g) cans cannellini beans, drained

6 cups (1.5 liters) water

Salt, to taste

2 bay leaves

1-in (2.5-cm) stick cinnamon

3 tablespoons oil

1 clove garlic, minced

1½ teaspoons cumin seeds

2 large tomatoes, finely chopped

2 fresh green chili peppers, deseeded and minced

1½ tablespoons peeled and minced fresh ginger

2 tablespoons ground coriander

1 teaspoon ground cumin

½ teaspoon ground turmeric

½ cup (125 g) nonfat plain yogurt, whisked until smooth

½ cup (20 g) fresh coriander leaves (cilantro), finely chopped

¼ teaspoon garam masala

1 If using dried cannellini beans, combine the beans, water, salt, bay leaves and cinnamon in a large saucepan. Bring to a boil, and then reduce the heat to low and simmer until the beans are tender, about 50 to 60 minutes, drain.

2 In a large saucepan, heat the oil over medium-high heat. Add the garlic and cook until golden, about 1 minute. Add the cumin seeds; they should sizzle upon contact with the hot oil. Add the tomatoes, green chili peppers and ginger, and cook, stirring constantly, initially over high and then over medium heat until all the juices evaporate, about 10 minutes.

3 Add the ground coriander, cumin and turmeric, and cook, stirring for 1 minute. Then add the yogurt a little at a time, stirring constantly to prevent it from curdling until it is absorbed. Mix in the cooked beans and fresh coriander and simmer uncovered for another 10 to 15 minutes, adding more water if necessary. Transfer to a serving dish, sprinkle the garam masala, and serve.

spicy red lentils

Serves **6**   Preparation **15 minutes**   Cooking **25 minutes**

Comfort food for many Indians, this preparation is simple to make yet very flavorful. When made a thinner consistency, it can be enjoyed as a soup. This is best had with a spicy relish like Coconut and Red Chili Sambal (page 20) and a helping of hot basmati rice.

1 cup (180 g) red lentils, rinsed and drained
4 cups (1 liter) water
¼ teaspoon ground turmeric
1 bay leaf
½ teaspoon salt, plus more to taste
2 tablespoons oil
1 small onion, finely chopped
½ tablespoon peeled and minced fresh ginger
½ tablespoon minced garlic
1 fresh green chili pepper, deseeded and minced
1 tablespoon ground coriander
½ teaspoon ground cumin
¼ teaspoon ground cinnamon
¼ teaspoon paprika
1 teaspoon sugar
3 tablespoons chopped fresh coriander leaves (cilantro)
3 tablespoons chopped fresh mint leaves
2 tablespoons fresh lemon juice

1 In a saucepan, combine the lentils, water, turmeric, bay leaf and salt. Bring to a boil, and then reduce the heat to medium and cook the lentils, stirring occasionally until they are tender but still firm, 12 to 15 minutes. Drain.

2 Heat the oil in a small skillet over medium heat. Add the onion, ginger, garlic, green chili pepper, ground coriander, cumin, cinnamon, paprika and sugar. Reduce the heat to low and cook until fragrant, about 2 minutes. Remove the pan from the heat.

3 Combine the lentils and spice mixture in a large bowl; toss gently to mix. Stir in fresh coriander and mint, and then the lemon juice. Serve immediately.

 ## madras style lentil and vegetable stew

Serves **6**   Preparation **15 minutes**   Cooking **50 minutes**

The spices and flavors used in this dish have a lot of curative value, and the turmeric in particular has several known benefits. This preparation can be served as a wholesome wellness soup, and it pairs well with any rice dish.

1 cup (180 g) dried lentils, rinsed and drained
6 cups (1.5 liters) water
¼ teaspoon ground turmeric
4 tablespoons oil
2 fresh green chili peppers, split lengthwise and deseeded
1 teaspoon black mustard seeds
¼ cup (25 g) fresh or frozen grated coconut
2 tablespoons minced fresh curry leaves
1 tablespoon peeled and minced fresh ginger
1 clove garlic, minced
4 cups (725 grams) mixed fresh vegetables, such as carrots, eggplant, green beans, and summer squash, cut into 1-in (2.5-cm) pieces
Salt, to taste
¼ cup (10 g) fresh coriander leaves (cilantro), chopped

1 Add the beans, water and turmeric to a large saucepan and bring to a boil. Reduce the heat to low, cover the saucepan, and cook, stirring occasionally until soft and creamy, 25 to 30 minutes. Stir vigorously to mash the beans. Keep warm.

2 Heat 2 tablespoons of the oil in a medium saucepan over medium-high heat and add the green chili peppers, mustard seeds, coconut and curry leaves. Add the ginger and garlic, and cook until softened, about 2 minutes. Pour it into the mashed lentils.

3 Add the remaining 2 tablespoons of oil, vegetables and salt to the same pan, and cook, stirring over medium-high heat until tender, about 8 to 10 minutes. Add the lentils and cook, stirring occasionally for about 10 minutes to blend the flavors. Add more water if needed. Serve hot, garnished with the fresh coriander.

hot and sour chickpeas

Serves **6** Preparation **15 minutes, plus 8 hours (dried bean soak time)** Cooking **1 hour**

This popular Indian street food with lightly spiced gravy is a hit when served with Indian breads. Serve this with Spinach and Thyme Roti Flatbreads (page 76) for a simple but delicious meal, or team it up with Cardamom Chicken (page 43) and Toasted Cumin Chapatis with Orange (page 72) for more elaborate fare.

3 tablespoons oil
1 tablespoon peeled and minced
   fresh ginger
2 tablespoons minced garlic
2 fresh green chili peppers,
   deseeded and minced
1 tablespoon ground coriander
2 teaspoons ground cumin
½ teaspoon garam masala
½ teaspoon chili powder
2 cups (320 g) dried chickpeas,
   washed, soaked overnight and
   drained, or one 16-oz (450-g) can
   chickpeas, drained and rinsed well
Salt, to taste
½ cup (125 ml) water
1 teaspoon cumin seeds
1-in (2.5-cm) piece fresh ginger,
   peeled and cut into matchsticks
1 small red onion, sliced
2 small tomatoes, diced
½ cup (20 g) fresh coriander leaves
   (cilantro), chopped

1 Heat 2 tablespoons of the oil in a large saucepan over medium-high heat and add the minced ginger, garlic and chili peppers. Stir until golden, about 1 minute. Add the coriander, cumin, garam masala and chili powder. Mix in the cooked chickpeas, salt and water, and cook, stirring as needed until tender and almost dry, about 5 minutes. Reduce the heat to medium, and cook another 5 minutes to blend the flavors. Transfer to a serving dish and keep warm.

2 Heat the remaining 1 tablespoon of oil in a small saucepan over medium-high heat and add the cumin seeds; they should sizzle upon contact with the hot oil. Quickly add the ginger matchsticks, and then add the onion and tomatoes and cook until golden. Stir about 1 minute and add to the chickpeas.

3 Garnish with the fresh coriander and serve hot.

yellow lentils with baby spinach and garlic

Serves 6   Preparation 15 minutes   Cooking 25 minutes

This is a very basic yellow dal that is made regularly in Indian homes. To add an interesting twist to this very common, workaday recipe, I've included Madras curry powder and coconut milk. Serve this with a portion of Crispy Southern Indian Fried Fish (page 66) and Saffron Rice with Toasted Almonds (page 73).

1 tablespoon oil
1 teaspoon black mustard seeds
1 onion, chopped
2 cloves garlic, crushed
1 teaspoon ground ginger
½ teaspoon Madras curry powder
1 cup (180 g) yellow lentils, rinsed
   and drained
1½ cups (375 ml) water
½ cup (125 ml) coconut milk
3 cups (225 g) baby spinach,
   chopped, or 1 cup (125 g) frozen
   chopped spinach, thawed
Salt, to taste
1 tablespoon chopped fresh
   coriander leaves (cilantro)
1 teaspoon sesame seeds

1 Heat the oil in a large saucepan over medium heat. Add the black mustard seeds; they should sizzle upon contact with the hot oil. Quickly add the onion, garlic, ginger and Madras curry powder, and cook stirring until the spices are fragrant, about 1 minute.
2 Add the lentils, water and coconut milk. Raise the heat to medium-high and bring it to boil. Reduce the heat to low, cover partially, and simmer until the lentils are tender but still firm, about 15 minutes.
3 Stir in the spinach and salt. Cover and simmer for about 3 minutes longer. Serve hot, garnished with fresh coriander and sesame seeds.

street-style spicy black chickpea masala

Serves 4 Preparation 15 minutes, plus 8 hours (dried bean soak time) Cooking 1 hour

I discovered this dish in western India while sampling local street food. Inspired, I conjured up similar flavors at home, but substituted dark red chili powder for a delectable smoky flavor. Use regular red chili powder if the Mexican variety is not available. Dried black chickpeas require a trip to an Indian grocery store—the canned variety is hard to find.

1½ cups (270 g) dried black chickpeas, rinsed, soaked overnight and drained
5 cups (1.25 liters) water
Salt, to taste
3 tablespoons clarified butter
1 teaspoon cumin seeds
2 onions, chopped
1 tablespoon peeled and minced fresh ginger
3 fresh green chili peppers, deseeded and minced
1 cup (225 g) finely-chopped tomatoes
5 green onions (scallions), finely chopped
1 tablespoon ground coriander
½ teaspoon dark red chili powder
1 tablespoon garam masala
¼ cup (10 g) fresh coriander leaves (cilantro), chopped
1 small red onion, thinly sliced
3 to 4 lime wedges, for garnish

1 Combine the chickpeas, water and salt in a large saucepan. Bring to a boil, then reduce the heat to low, cover partially and simmer until the chickpeas are tender, about 45 minutes. Drain and reserve.

2 Heat the clarified butter in a large saucepan over medium-high heat. Add the cumin seeds; they should sizzle upon contact with the hot oil. Add the chopped onions and cook until dark golden brown, stirring frequently to prevent sticking. Add water if necessary.

3 Add the ginger and green chili peppers, tomatoes and green onions, and cook for about 3 to 5 minutes. Mix in the ground coriander, dark red chili powder, and garam masala.

4 Add the chickpeas and cook on high heat until all the water evaporates and the chickpeas are glazed with a dark brown coating, about 10 to 15 minutes. Serve topped with the fresh coriander, red onion slices, and lime wedges.

red bean ragout with plum tomatoes and thyme

Serves 6 Preparation 15 minutes Cooking 25 minutes

Rajma, or the red kidney bean, is a very common legume in northern Indian kitchens. When prepared as a stew, or ragout, and eaten with hot plain rice, it is known as rajma-chawal. I have used fresh thyme, instead of the typical fresh coriander (cilantro), to give this dish an altogether new dimension.

2 tablespoons oil

1 teaspoon cumin seeds

2 onions, minced

1½ teaspoons chopped fresh
     thyme leaves

2 teaspoons peeled and minced
     fresh ginger

4 cloves garlic, minced

2 fresh green chili peppers,
     deseeded and minced

2 large plum tomatoes, chopped

2 teaspoons ground coriander

1 teaspoon ground cumin

¼ teaspoon ground turmeric

1 teaspoon garam masala

One 16-oz (450-g) can kidney
     beans, drained and rinsed

2 cups (500 ml) water

Salt, to taste

2 sprigs fresh thyme

1 Heat the oil in a large saucepan over medium-high heat. Add the cumin seeds and let them sizzle. Quickly add the onion and chopped thyme, and cook, stirring frequently until the onions begin to brown, about 5 minutes.

2 Add the ginger, garlic, green chili peppers, tomatoes, coriander, cumin, turmeric and garam masala, and fry until the oil separates, about 5 minutes.

3 Add the red kidney beans, the water and salt, and cook until the beans are tender and the flavors are well blended, about 10 minutes. Mash some of the beans roughly; this thickens the sauce. Transfer to a large serving bowl and serve garnished with the sprigs of thyme.

Chapter Eight

vegetables, eggs and cheese

 Indians have truly perfected the art of vegetarian cooking. From the simplest of vegetables, Indian cooks create a mouth-watering variety of food. And so, the trend toward healthy living is encouraging many Americans to join the "vegetarian revolution." To avoid giving up taste, appearance and variety in the foods that they eat, many vegetarians turn to Indian cuisine for inspiration. Using spices, seasonings and nutritious ingredients such as leafy vegetables, grains, fruits and legumes, Indian vegetarian dishes have unique, interesting and satisfying flavors.

Vegetable dishes are a key part of every Indian meal, whether for vegetarians or meat eaters. Typically, vegetables are either braised or sautéed, combined with garlic and spices, and served with rice or curries.

The *thali*—literally meaning a "plate," but denoting a set meal, sometimes with unlimited servings—is a style of serving food that's almost synonymous with vegetarian fare. An endless procession of fresh vegetables cooked in aromatic spices, a variety of crisp, fried snacks, staples like rice and rotis, and an array of delectable confections typically appear in the *thali*. Serve several simple vegetable and cheese dishes included in this chapter in small portions and delight your friends and family with a *thali* dinner on any special occasion!

Eggs are not considered part of a vegetarian diet in India like they are in the West. Here you will find two familiar egg recipes with an Indian twist. Indian herbs and spices and ingredients like ginger, chili and tomato are used to add spice and flavor.

baby beets and carrots with curry leaves

Serves 4   Preparation **15 minutes**   Cooking **30 minutes**

This recipe brings back some very warm memories of one of my favorite places in New York City—the Farmer's Market at Union Square. The sight is always so spectacular—it is often my therapy for a tired soul! I discovered a variety of differently colored baby beets there, and ever since I have experimented with using them as ingredients in several of my dishes. Here, I have used red and yellow baby beets. The dash of rice vinegar and the curry leaves add to the robust and heady flavor of this dish.

1 lb (500 g) red and yellow beets
½ lb (250 g) baby carrots, peeled
1 tablespoon oil
8 fresh curry leaves
2 tablespoons deseeded and minced fresh green chili peppers
3 tablespoons minced shallots
1 tablespoon rice vinegar
Salt, to taste
1 teaspoon sugar

1 If the beet greens are still attached, cut them off, leaving about 1 in (2.5 cm) of stem intact. Bring 1 in (2.5 cm) of water to a boil in a large pot. Add the unpeeled beets, cover, and cook until tender, 20 to 25 minutes. Remove from the pot and let it stand until cool enough to handle, then peel and cut into quarters. Set

aside and keep warm.
2 Cook the baby carrots the same way you cooked the beets. (If the baby carrots are various sizes, cut the larger ones into halves or thirds for even cooking). Remove from the pot and set aside.
3 Place a pan over medium-high heat. Add the oil and, when it is hot, add the curry leaves, chili

peppers and shallots. Cook for 2 to 3 minutes, stirring occasionally. Add the beets and carrots and stir. Add the vinegar, salt, and sugar and stir well. Raise the heat to high and stir-fry for 2 to 3 minutes.
4 Remove from the heat and taste for seasoning. Transfer to a serving dish and serve hot or at room temperature.

oven-roasted spiced eggplant

Serves 6   Preparation **10 minutes**   Cooking **20 minutes**

The eggplants used in this recipe are not the typical large ones—often referred to as the "globe" variety—that are commonly found supermarkets. Here, I use the long, slim eggplants that can be found in Asian or Indian markets, and which deliver a slightly different flavor when cooked than the larger, common ones. This preparation is rather simple and healthy, yet the touch of cumin and green chili peppers makes it really tasty. This can easily be stuffed in Indian flatbreads or a store-bought wrap for a perfect meal-on-the-go.

4 medium-sized purple Asian eggplants

½ **cup (125 ml) oil**

½ **teaspoon salt, plus more, to taste**

1 **large onion, thinly sliced**

1 **teaspoon minced garlic**

½ **teaspoon ground cayenne pepper**

½ **teaspoon ground turmeric**

½ **teaspoon cumin seeds, toasted and coarsely ground (page 7)**

2 **tablespoons deseeded and minced green chili peppers**

2 **tablespoons minced green onions (scallions)**

¼ **cup (10 g) fresh coriander leaves (cilantro), for garnish**

1 Preheat the oven to 450°F (230°C).
2 Cut the eggplant into 1-in (2.5-cm) dice. Lightly toss the eggplant with ¼ cup (65 ml) of the oil and ½ teaspoon of salt. Place the eggplant on a baking sheet or roasting pan and bake in the center of the oven until lightly brown and the flesh is softened, about 10 minutes. Remove from the oven and set aside.

3 Heat the remaining ¼ cup (65ml) oil in a heavy skillet over medium-high heat. Add the onion, garlic, chili powder, turmeric and cumin, and stir to mix well. Lower the heat to medium and cook, stirring frequently until the onion is well softened and translucent but not browned, about 10 minutes.

4 Add the chili peppers to the onion mixture and sauté for about a minute. Then add the roasted eggplant and salt to taste, and gently stir the ingredients together using spatula.

5 Just before serving, stir in the green onions. Garnish with coriander leaves and serve hot or cold.

mustard potatoes with dill

Serves **6**   Preparation **10 minutes**   Cooking **25 minutes**

Simple to make and yet delicious, this versatile potato dish can be cooked up with spinach if dill is not readily available in your fridge. Serve it with hot chapatis and Mango and Roasted Red Pepper Chutney (page 23) for a simple yet wholesome family meal at home.

1 lb (500 g) potatoes, diced
¼ cup (65 ml) oil
5 cloves garlic, minced
2 teaspoons black mustard seeds
2 dried red chili peppers
1 tablespoon Madras curry powder
6 cups (100 g) fresh dill, chopped
Salt, to taste

1 Boil the potatoes in a saucepan over medium-high heat for 10 to 15 minutes, or until just tender. Drain well.

2 Heat the oil in a heavy-bottomed saucepan over medium-high heat. Add the garlic and fry for 30 seconds. Add the mustard seeds and the chili peppers, cover, and briefly allow the seeds to pop. Stir in the potatoes with the curry powder and sauté until fragrant. Add the dill, cover, and cook over low heat for 5 minutes. Season with salt and serve hot.

aromatic butternut squash

Serves 4   Preparation **15 minutes**   Cooking **20 minutes**

This dish is traditionally made with jaggery, but for the sake of convenience—without compromising the authenticity of the taste—I have used brown sugar. Grated coconut adds a wonderful dimension to the texture and flavor of this slightly sweetened butternut squash dish. These very same ingredients are used in Butternut Squash Soup with Exotic Spices (page 34), but there the squash is puréed with coconut milk. This can be served with Basmati Rice with Dry-Roasted Spices (page 77).

2 tablespoons oil

½ teaspoon cumin seeds

2 dried red chili peppers, stemmed

1-in (2.5-cm) cinnamon stick

2 bay leaves

1 cup (150 g) chopped onion

1 lb (500 g) butternut squash, peeled and diced

1 teaspoon ground coriander seeds

1 teaspoon brown sugar

Salt, to taste

1 cup (100 g) fresh or frozen grated coconut

¼ cup (65 ml) water

¼ cup (10 g) fresh coriander leaves (cilantro), chopped

1 Heat the oil in a large heavy skillet over medium-high heat. Add the cumin seeds, red chili peppers, cinnamon stick and bay leaves, and fry briefly. Add the onion and cook, stirring frequently until golden brown, about 5 minutes.

2 Add the squash, lower the heat to medium, and cook, stirring constantly to prevent sticking, for 5 minutes. Add the ground coriander, brown sugar and salt, and cook until the squash is softened.

3 Add the grated coconut and stir to break up any lumps and blend it into the squash. Add the water and cook for 2 to 3 minutes, stirring to prevent sticking. Taste for seasoning and adjust if necessary. Garnish with the chopped fresh coriander leaves.

stir-fried potatoes and green beans with mint

Serves 6   Preparation **15 minutes**   Cooking **30 minutes**

This one's a perfect home-style subzi, or vegetable dish. Traditionally one would use chopped fresh coriander for this dish. I like to use mint to give this everyday food an interesting twist. Combine it with Spinach and Thyme Roti Flatbreads (page 76) and a portion of Spicy Red Lentils (page 87) for a perfect Indian meal.

8 potatoes (about 4 lbs/1.75 kg total), washed
½ lb (500 g) green beans
3 tablespoons oil
1 tablespoon black mustard seeds
1 tablespoon cumin seeds
1 teaspoon ground turmeric
2 tomatoes, coarsely chopped
Salt, to taste
2 fresh green chili peppers, deseeded and minced
4 green onions (scallions), minced
¼ cup (2 g) mint leaves, chopped

1 Place the potatoes in a large pot with cold water to cover, bring to a boil, and cook until just cooked through but still very firm (test the largest potato in the pot; it should be firm but cooked at the center). Drain and set aside to cool.

2 Meanwhile, bring water to a boil in a medium pot. Toss in the green beans and cook until just tender, about 8–10 minutes. Drain, rinse under cold water to cool, and then drain again. Trim, cut into ½-in (1.25-cm) lengths, and set aside.

3 Peel the potatoes and cut them into 1-in (2.5-cm) dice. Set aside.

4 Heat the oil in a wok or a wide heavy pot over medium-high heat. When the oil is hot, toss in the mustard seeds. When they stop popping, add the cumin seeds and turmeric, stir briefly, and then stir in the tomatoes and salt. Stir-fry for about 1 minute. Add the potatoes and stir-fry for another minute. Stir in the chili peppers, green onions, green beans and mint. Remove from the heat, taste for salt, and adjust if necessary. Serve hot.

green cabbage with lentils

Serves 6   Preparation 15 minutes   Cooking 30 minutes

While growing up in southern India, this was easily one of the simplest comfort foods in my family. Homey, easy to make, and quicker to serve, my version uses most of the traditional ingredients that my family used when making this dish. And fortunately all of them can be found at your local grocer's. I like to keep the cabbage for a minimal time on the heat so that it retains its crunchiness. For truly no-hassle, easy-to-make dinner or lunch fare, serve this with any of the rice dishes and Spicy Red Lentils (page 87).

1 cup (180 g) dried lentils

2 tablespoons oil

1¼ teaspoons cumin seeds

8 fresh curry leaves

1 tablespoon peeled and minced fresh ginger

1 tablespoon minced garlic

2 fresh green chili peppers, deseeded and minced

1 teaspoon ground coriander

1 small head green cabbage (about 1¼ lbs/600 g), finely shredded

Salt, to taste

½ cup (10 g) fresh coriander leaves (cilantro), including soft stems, chopped

¼ teaspoon garam masala

1 Wash the lentils and add them to a pot of boiling water. Cook until soft, about 12 to 15 minutes. Make sure it does not get too soft and mushy.

2 Heat the oil in a large saucepan over medium-high heat and add the cumin seeds and curry leaves; they should sizzle upon contact with the hot oil. Quickly add the ginger, garlic, green chili peppers and ground coriander, and cook, stirring, about 2 minutes.

3 Add the cabbage and salt, cover the pan, and cook, stirring as needed over medium-high heat for 2 to 3 minutes. Then reduce the heat to medium-low heat and cook until the cabbage is tender, about 10 minutes.

4 Mix in the cooked lentils and fresh coriander during the last 5 minutes of cooking. Transfer to a serving bowl, sprinkle the garam masala on top, and serve.

masala scrambled eggs with crumbled paneer

Serves **6**   Preparation **5 minutes**   Cooking **5 minutes**

This is a slightly Indianized version of scrambled eggs with cheese, served universally at home and in diners across the country. I have used Indian paneer and some fresh coriander (cilantro) to give this popular egg preparation a new twist. You can use this scramble in a wrap and make it a to-go meal in minutes.

2 tablespoons oil
1 small onion, chopped
1 large tomato, chopped
2 fresh green chili peppers, deseeded and minced
1 tablespoon peeled and minced fresh ginger
1 tablespoon fresh lemon juice
Salt, to taste
6 large eggs, lightly beaten
1 cup (150 g) paneer cheese, coarsely crumbled
1 tablespoon chopped fresh coriander leaves (cilantro)

1 Heat the oil in a large non-stick saucepan over medium-high heat. Add the onion, tomato and green chili peppers, and cook, stirring until most of the tomato juices are dry, about 5 minutes. Stir in the ginger, lemon juice and salt.
2 Add the eggs and cook over medium heat, stirring constantly until firm, about 2 minutes.
3 Mix in the paneer cheese and fresh coriander. Serve hot.

spice stuffed okra

Serves **6**   Preparation **20 minutes**   Cooking **30 minutes**

This recipe is a little more elaborate than the simplest okra preparations. But, mark my words—the work will be worth it. This is by far one of the tastiest ways of using okra in Indian cuisine.

1½ lbs (750 g) fresh, tender okra, rinsed and patted dry
3 tablespoons oil
1½ teaspoons cumin seeds
1 large onion, cut in half lengthwise and thinly sliced
1 large tomato, coarsely chopped

Masala
1 tablespoon ground coriander
1 teaspoon ground cumin
1 teaspoon mango powder
1 teaspoon ground fennel seeds
½ teaspoon ground turmeric
½ teaspoon garam masala
¼ teaspoon ground paprika
¼ teaspoon Asian chili powder or ground cayenne pepper
Salt, to taste

1 Make the Masala by mixing the spices and salt together in a small bowl.
2 Cut off the end of the okra stem and discard. Make a long slit on one side from the stem down, stopping ¾-in (2-cm) from the tip. (This forms a stuffing pocket, but keeps the okra intact.) Stuff ¼ to ½ teaspoon of the spice mixture into each okra pocket. Reserve any leftover spice mixture.
3 Heat 2 tablespoons of the oil over medium-high heat in a non-stick skillet and add the cumin seeds; they should sizzle upon contact with the hot oil. Quickly add the onion and cook, stirring until golden, about 5 minutes. Transfer to a bowl, leaving behind any oil.
4 Lay all the stuffed okra in the skillet in a single layer. Drizzle the remaining 1 tablespoon oil on top and cook over medium-low heat, turning the pieces very carefully, until golden brown, about 10 to 15 minutes. Scatter the cooked onions over the okra and then add any leftover spices. Mix carefully and cook over medium-low heat, turning occasionally, about 5 minutes. Transfer to a serving dish.
5 Add the tomato to the skillet and cook over high heat until wilted and coated with spices left in the skillet, about 2 minutes. Transfer to the okra platter and serve.

southern indian masala with potatoes and peas

Serves 6   Preparation **15 minutes**   Cooking **35 minutes**

I love tarragon. It is a very versatile herb and spruces up a dish beautifully. And though it is not at all a conventional Indian ingredient, it works wonderfully in some typical Indian dishes because of the fresh flowery scent it adds. Using dried tarragon is never a comparable substitute for the fresh variety. If fresh tarragon is not available, use an equal amount of fresh coriander (cilantro) rather than dried tarragon flakes. The curry leaves lend a perfect balance of bitterness and sweetness in this southern Indian vegetable dish.

1 lb (500 g) small red or white
   potatoes
3 tablespoons oil
1 teaspoon black mustard seeds
1 tablespoon dried yellow split
   chickpeas
1 red onion, thinly sliced
1 tablespoon ground coriander
¼ teaspoon red pepper flakes
¼ teaspoon ground turmeric
2 tablespoons minced fresh curry
   leaves
2 fresh green chili peppers,
   deseeded and minced
1 cup (150 g) frozen peas, thawed
Salt to taste
½ cup (20 g) fresh tarragon,
   chopped

1 Put the potatoes in a saucepan, add water to cover, and bring to a boil over high heat. Reduce the heat to medium and cook, uncovered, until the potatoes are tender, 15 to 20 minutes. Drain and let stand until cool enough to handle. Cut each potato into quarters. Set aside.

2 Heat the oil in large non-stick wok or skillet over medium-high heat and add the mustard seeds and chickpeas. The seeds should splutter upon contact with the oil, so cover the pan for safety and reduce the heat to medium until the spluttering subsides.

3 Quickly add the onion and cook, stirring until golden, about 5 minutes. Then mix in the coriander, red pepper flakes, turmeric, curry leaves and green chili peppers. Cook for 1 minute, and then add the potatoes, peas and salt. Cover and cook, stirring occasionally, over medium-low heat until the potatoes are golden, 5 to 7 minutes. Add then tarragon and transfer to a serving dish.

mixed rainbow vegetables with kadhai paneer

Serves 6   Preparation 20 minutes   Cooking 15 minutes

In a traditional preparation of kadhai paneer, the masala and the spices are ground into a wet paste. However, in this recipe, I call for a stir-fried variety of the same spices that go into the making of the traditional kadhai paneer. Adding the various bell peppers makes the dish a visual treat. This is also one of those recipes that requires minimal prep time and yet becomes a delight on the table.

3 tablespoons oil
1 tablespoon peeled and minced fresh ginger
2 large cloves garlic, minced
2 small onions, diced
1 tablespoon ground coriander
1 teaspoon ground cumin
½ teaspoon ground fennel seeds
½ teaspoon ground cardamom seeds
½ teaspoon red pepper flakes
Salt, to taste
4 small tomatoes, diced
2 small green bell peppers, deseeded and diced
2 small red bell peppers, deseeded and diced
2 small yellow bell peppers, deseeded and diced
6 oz (170 g) paneer cheese, diced
4 tablespoons chopped fresh coriander leaves (cilantro)
4 green onions (scallions), chopped
Freshly-ground black pepper, to taste

1 Heat the oil in a large non-stick wok or skillet over medium-high heat, and then add the ginger and garlic and briefly cook, stirring, about 1 minute. Add the onions and cook, stirring until golden, 2 to 3 minutes.

2 Reduce the heat to medium and add the coriander, cumin, fennel, cardamom, red pepper flakes and salt, and stir for about 2 minutes. Add the tomatoes and bell peppers, cover, and continue to cook, stirring constantly until the dish is saucy, about 5 minutes.

3 Add the paneer, fresh coriander and green onions, and increase to medium-high heat. Cook uncovered for about 5 minutes. Serve hot, sprinkled with black pepper.

masala petit pois with baby carrots and coconut

Serves 6   Preparation 10 minutes   Cooking 15 minutes

This dish is proof that you can quickly and easily prepare a delicious Indian dish using ingredients that are probably already in your freezer!

1 lb (500 g) fresh shelled or frozen green peas
5 tablespoons oil
1 lb (500 g) diced frozen carrots
2¼ cups (550 ml) water
¾ cup (75 g) grated fresh or frozen coconut
¼ cup (40 g) cashew nuts
2 teaspoons cumin seeds
1 teaspoon black mustard seeds
1 onion, chopped
1 tablespoon peeled and minced fresh ginger
1 clove garlic, minced
2 teaspoons ground coriander
1 teaspoon Asian chili powder or ground cayenne pepper
1 teaspoon ground turmeric
Salt, to taste
1 tomato, chopped
5 fresh curry leaves
2 cups (500 ml) water
3 tablespoons chopped fresh coriander leaves (cilantro)

1 If using fresh peas, boil the fresh peas with water to cover in a large saucepan until tender and soft. Drain. If using frozen peas, thaw.
2 Heat 2 tablespoons of the oil in a large saucepan over medium-high heat. Add the carrots and sauté for 3 minutes; set aside.
3 Put ¼ cup (65 ml) of the water, the coconut, and cashew nuts in a blender and process to a fine paste.
4 Heat the remaining 3 tablespoons of oil in a large saucepan over medium-high heat. Add the cumin seeds and black mustard seeds and sauté until fragrant, about 1 minute.
5 Add the onion, ginger and garlic, and sauté until light brown, about 2 to 3 minutes. Stir in the ground coriander, Asian chili powder, turmeric and salt. Add tomatoes and sauté until the fat leaves the mixture, about 5 minutes.
6 Reduce the heat to medium, add the coconut and cashew paste and the curry leaves, and cook for a minute, stirring.
7 Add the remaining 2 cups (500 ml) of water and bring it to a boil. Add the peas and carrots, reduce the heat, and simmer for 5 minutes. Serve hot, garnished with the chopped fresh coriander.

spicy bombay chili eggs with broccolini

Serves 6   Preparation 5 minutes   Cooking 5 minutes

This dish is welcome on both the breakfast and lunch menus! Broccolini, a vegetable that can be consumed in its entirety, tastes like a cross between broccoli and asparagus. If not available at your local grocer's, seek it out at an Asian market. If you can't find broccolini, substitute broccoli. For the health-conscious, try this recipe with egg whites only. Serve it with hot Toasted Cumin Chapatis with Orange (page 72) for a light, yet tasty meal.

6 large eggs
½ teaspoon ground cumin
½ teaspoon salt
Freshly-ground black pepper, to taste
2 tablespoons oil
3 fresh green chili peppers, deseeded and minced
6 green onions (scallions), minced
1 teaspoon peeled and minced fresh ginger
½ lb (250 g) broccolini, chopped
1 large tomato, chopped
1 teaspoon ground turmeric
2 tablespoons chopped fresh coriander leaves (cilantro)

1 Beat the eggs in a large bowl with the cumin, salt and pepper. Heat the oil in a large non-stick skillet over medium heat. Add the chili peppers, green onions, ginger and broccolini. Cook, stirring constantly until soft, about 5 minutes.
2 Add the tomato and turmeric and cook for 2 minutes.
3 Add the eggs and cook on medium heat until firm (but not dry), about 3 minutes, stirring constantly. Once the eggs have congealed, transfer them to a serving platter. Serve hot, garnished with coriander leaves.

homemade paneer cheese

Makes ½ lb (225 g)   Preparation **10 minutes**   Cooking **30 minutes**

Paneer, also known as Indian cottage cheese, is made by curdling milk with something sour, such as yogurt, lemon juice or vinegar, and then separating the curds from the whey. This soft, spongy cheese with its sweet, milky aroma is preservative-free, has no artificial additives, and can be made with low-fat or whole milk. Paneer cheese can be served as part of an antipasto platter, giving it an Italian twist with salt, pepper, chopped fresh basil and balsamic vinegar or as a caprese salad with fresh plum tomato and basil.

½ **gallon (2 liters) low-fat or whole milk**
½ **cup (125 ml) fresh lemon juice**
2-**ft (60-cm) square piece of fine muslin or layers of cheesecloth**

1 Place the milk in a large, heavy saucepan and heat, stirring constantly, over medium-high heat. Just before the milk comes to a boil, add the lemon juice and continue to stir until the milk curdles and separates into curds and whey, 1 to 2 minutes. Remove from the heat. Let the mixture sit for 5 minutes.
2 Drape the muslin or cheesecloth over a strainer and place both over a large pot to catch the whey. Pour the cheese curds and whey into the muslin-lined strainer. Tie the ends of the cloth together and hang to drain over a sink. Allow to drain 3 to 5 minutes.

3 Twist the cloth around the cheese to press out excess whey, then place the cheese between two plates. Place a large pan of water or a heavy saucepan on the top plate and let the cheese drain further, 10 to 20 minutes.
4 Take the weight off the cheese (which, by now, should have compressed into a chunk), cut the cheese into desired shapes and sizes and use as needed. Store in an airtight container in the refrigerator 4 to 5 days or freeze up to 4 months.

Variation Paneer cheese can also be made with about 1 cup (80 g) fresh chopped herbs, such as basil, tarragon or mint.

zucchini with yellow mung lentils and roasted garlic

Serves 6   Preparation 15 minutes   Cooking 40 minutes

The combination of lentils, vegetables, garlic and cumin gives this satisfying side dish a unique flavor that goes perfectly with all sorts of main dishes. If zucchini is not available, use other common squashes such as summer squash (ghía) or calabash, also known as "bottle gourd" (doodhi). The addition of lentils in this side dish makes it a nutritious main dish for vegetarians when paired with rice or bread and a raita or plain yogurt.

1 cup (180 g) yellow mung lentils, rinsed and drained
½ teaspoon ground turmeric
¼ teaspoon of salt
4 cups (1 liter) water
2 tablespoons oil
6 cloves garlic, crushed
1 teaspoon cumin seeds
1 small onion, thinly sliced
4 small zucchini, cut into ¼-in (6-mm) slices
1 tablespoon ground coriander
1 tablespoon ground cumin
½ teaspoon ground paprika
2 tablespoons chopped fresh coriander (cilantro)
1 teaspoon garam masala

1 Put the lentils into a large saucepan with the turmeric, salt and water. Bring to a boil and skim well. Reduce the heat and simmer, covered, until the lentils are cooked, about 15 to 20 minutes. Drain the lentils and transfer to a serving bowl. Cover the bowl and keep warm.

2 Heat the oil in a medium saucepan over over medium heat. Add the garlic and cook until golden brown and well roasted.

3 Add the cumin seeds; they should sizzle upon contact with the hot oil. Quickly add the onion and zucchini and cook for 10 to 15 minutes.

4 Add the coriander and cumin and cook for 10 minutes, or until the zucchini is cooked.

5 Remove the pan from the heat, add the paprika, and immediately pour over the hot lentils, swirling lightly to mix. Sprinkle the fresh coriander and garam masala on top and serve.

sweet and sour asparagus with cashews

Serves 6   Preparation 20 minutes   Cooking 30 minutes

Most of the produce at your local grocery can be incorporated into tasty and simply-made Indian fare. Take asparagus. It is not a conventional Indian ingredient, but when prepared with Indian spices, as in this dish, it's given a whole new dimension. In fact, it's given a royal makeover! Serve this healthy dish with the Honey Roasted Stuffed Lamb (page 53) for a complete and perfect meal.

1 lb (500 g) asparagus, trimmed and cut into 2-in (5-cm) pieces
3 tablespoons oil
½ teaspoon cumin seeds
½ teaspoon black mustard seeds
2 small onions, sliced
1 tablespoon peeled and minced fresh ginger
1 large clove garlic, minced
2 fresh green chili peppers, deseeded and chopped
1 tablespoon ground coriander
½ teaspoon ground cumin
Salt, to taste
1 large tomato, coarsely chopped
¼ cup (60 g) nonfat plain yogurt, whisked until smooth
½ cup (75 g) cashew nuts, toasted and coarsely chopped (page 7)
¼ teaspoon garam masala

1 Parcook the asparagus in boiling water in a wide pan or in a microwave for about 2 to 3 minutes. Chill in ice water, drain and set aside.
2 Heat the oil in a medium non-stick wok or saucepan over medium-high heat, and then add the cumin and black mustard seeds; they should sizzle upon contact with the hot oil. Quickly add the onions and cook, stirring until golden brown, about 5 minutes.
3 Add the ginger, garlic and green chili peppers and stir for about 1 minute, and then stir in the coriander, cumin and salt.
4 Add the tomato and cook until lightly soft, about 1 minute.
5 Add the yogurt, stirring constantly to prevent it from curdling, about 2 minutes.
6 Add the asparagus and cook until the flavors are well blended, about 2 minutes.
7 Serve garnished with toasted cashew nuts and sprinkle garam masala on top.

paneer picatta

Serves 6   Preparation **10 minutes**   Cooking **5 minutes**

This dish was inspired by picatta, an Italian word that describes a particular manner of cooking. The most commonly prepared picatta dish in this country is made with chicken or fish that has been sliced across its width and sautéed in butter with Italian spices and parsley. Paneer, an Indian cheese, is a very versatile ingredient, and its capacity to absorb the flavors in which it marinates makes it one of my favorite main course recipes for vegetarians. The ginger and chili peppers give this dish the boost that an Indian dish requires. The use of fresh coriander (cilantro) instead of parsley also adds to the uniqueness of this picatta-style dish. Enjoy it with a simple pasta or either a portion of Mint Pilaf with Potatoes and Cumin (page 78) or Basmati Rice with Dry-Roasted Spices (page 77).

8 oz (250 g) paneer cheese, cut into 1-in (2.5-cm) thick square pieces

Salt, to taste

Freshly-ground black pepper, to taste

1 tablespoon oil

¼ cup (65 ml) sherry or dry white wine

1 small onion, minced

¼ cup (45 g) drained capers

1 tablespoon peeled and minced fresh ginger

2 fresh green chili peppers, deseeded and minced

Juice of 1 lemon

2 tablespoons butter

4 tablespoons chopped fresh coriander leaves (cilantro)

1 Season the paneer lightly with salt and black pepper.

2 Heat the oil in a large non-stick skillet or griddle over medium-high heat and quickly sear the paneer cheese pieces until golden, about 30 seconds per side. Transfer to a serving dish, cover and keep warm.

3 Add the sherry or wine to deglaze the pan, and scrape the browned bits off the bottom of the pan.

4 Add the onion, capers, ginger and green chili peppers, and cook, stirring, for about 2 minutes. Add the lemon juice, butter and fresh coriander, and then drizzle the mixture over the paneer pieces. Serve hot.

desserts and drinks

 Exquisite desserts and sweets are an integral part of Indian cuisine, and comprise the perfect ending to a meal. Indian sweets aid in digestion, particularly after spicy meals. In India, sweets are generally called *mithai*, which refers to confections made with sugar, milk and condensed milk that are prepared by deep-frying. Indian desserts are often embellished with cardamom, raisins, almonds, pistachios, cashews and fruit such as mangoes, guavas, pineapple, melon, cherries, oranges and bananas. The recipes in this chapter have been adapted from traditional Indian desserts, but with a contemporary twist, so that they can be made by anyone.

The drinks that are served in India are quite different from those in any other part of the world, each having its special Indian touch. They range from ginger-infused lemonades, hot tea and milk laced with cardamom, or frothy yogurt blended with ice and freshly crushed cumin seeds. Most consist of natural ingredients like fruits, milk, sugarcane and so on.

During summer months, most parts of India are hot and dry; to quench one's thirst, what's needed are light, cold and refreshing beverages. Summer fruits such as watermelon, mango, lichee, sweet lime, musk melon, oranges, papaya, grapes, coconut, pineapples and pomegranate are popular ingredients. You can add carbonated drinks or even alcohol to some of these drinks to jazz up the taste! The drinks in this chapter can be served with any meal and go well with all Indian foods.

sweet yogurt sundae with saffron and pistachios

Serves 8   **Preparation 10 minutes, plus 3 hours for draining**

The most vital step in preparing this dish is to drain the yogurt long enough to eliminate much of the moisture from it. This is the secret to a perfect shrikhand, as this drained and sweetened yogurt dessert is known in India. What follows is a recipe for a basic shrikhand. Using your imagination, there is no end to the variety of ways it can be presented. For example, you can layer it with seasonal fruit compotes, crushed berries, and chocolate ganache and serve it either in shot glasses or build it into an interesting parfait.

2 feet (60 cm) square piece of fine muslin or layers of cheesecloth
4 cups (975 g) plain whole milk yogurt
1 teaspoon saffron strands
⅓ cup (80 ml) whole milk
1 teaspoon ground cardamom
¼ teaspoon freshly-ground nutmeg
½ cup (125 ml) honey
¼ cup (35 g) coarsely-chopped pistachios

1 Line a large sieve or colander with muslin or cheesecloth. Wet the cloth with water, then place the muslin-lined sieve or colander over a bowl. Place the yogurt in the sieve to drain for 2 to 3 hours in the refrigerator. Discard the whey.

2 Turn the yogurt into a bowl and set aside.

3 Lightly toast the saffron strands in small dry skillet over medium heat, until brittle. Add the milk, cardamom and nutmeg. Remove from the heat and stir in the honey until dissolved.

4 Whisk the mixture into the yogurt. Use a ladle to pour the yogurt into glasses, sundae cups or bowls. Top with nuts and serve chilled.

chocolate-ginger cake with dates

Serves 8   Preparation **10 minutes**   Cooking **25 minutes**

Although not commonly known, the flavors of ginger and chocolate complement each other very well. Besides being delicious, this recipe is very flexible. I have used dates, but you could make this using any other dried fruits with equally good results. And you can make individual portion sizes using muffin tins—viola, cupcakes!

9 oz (260 g) bittersweet chocolate, chopped

1 cup, plus 2 tablespoons (2¼ sticks/250 g) unsalted butter at room temperature, plus extra for buttering pan

1 cup (200 g) sugar

4 large eggs, at room temperature

½ cup, plus 1 tablespoon (80 g) all-purpose flour, plus extra for dusting pan

2 teaspoon ginger powder

¼ cup (85 g) moist dates, such as Medjool, cut into small pieces

1 Preheat the oven to 350ºF (175ºC). Butter the inside of a 9-in (23-cm) square cake pan. Line the bottom with parchment paper, butter the paper and dust with flour; tap out the excess and set the pan aside.

2 Melt the chocolate in a bowl over simmering water or place the chocolate in a bowl and melt it in a microwave oven. Set the chocolate aside to cool. It should feel only just warm to touch when it is mixed with the rest of the ingredients.

3 Put the butter and sugar in the bowl of a mixer fitted with the paddle attachment and beat on medium speed for about 5 minutes, scraping down the sides of the bowl frequently until the butter is creamy and the sugar well blended into it. Add the eggs one at a time, beating for 1 minute after each addition. Reduce the mixer speed to low and pour in the cooled chocolate.

4 Add the flour, ginger and dates, and mix into the batter at medium speed.

5 Scrape the batter into the pan, smooth the top, and slide the pan into the oven. Bake for 20 to 25 minutes or until the cake rises slightly; the top may crack a bit and the cake may not entirely set in center when done. To test the cake for doneness, insert a slender knife into the center; the knife will come out slightly streaked with batter, which is what you want. Transfer the cake to a rack to cool.

6 When the cake is completely cooled, chill it in the refrigerator for an hour or two to make it easy to unmold. Turn the cake out, remove the parchment, and invert the cake onto a serving platter so that it is right side up. Allow the cake to come to room temperature before slicing and serving.

orange and saffron yogurt cake

Makes **1 loaf**   Preparation **10 minutes**   Cooking **40 minutes**

The two main flavors used in this dessert—orange and saffron—give it a very fresh and summery taste. It is particularly good when served with ice cream or fruit compote (or both!), and it freezes quite well.

½ cup, plus 2 tablespoons (275 g) plain whole yogurt
1 cup plus 2 tablespoon (225 g) sugar
2 teaspoons saffron strands
2 large eggs
½ cup (125 ml) oil
Finely-grated zest of 1 lemon
Juice of 1 lemon
Finely-grated zest of 2 oranges
Juice of 1 orange
½ vanilla bean, split and scraped
1 cup, plus 2 tablespoons (150 g) all-purpose flour
2¼ teaspoons baking powder

1 Preheat the oven to 350ºF (175ºC). Butter the inside of a 9 x 5 x 3-in (23 x 12.5 x 7.5-cm) loaf pan.
2 In a large bowl, whisk together the yogurt, sugar, saffron, and eggs. Add the oil, lemon zest, lemon juice, orange zest, orange juice and vanilla bean seeds. Add the flour and baking powder, whisking until just combined. Do not over mix.
3 Pour the batter into prepared pan. Bake until a knife inserted into the center of the cake comes out clean, 30 to 40 minutes. The cake will be dark golden on top and should pull away just a bit from the sides of the pan. If the crust begins to darken too much, cover the cake with a piece of aluminum foil. Cool in the pan on a wire rack for 10 minutes. Invert the cake onto a wire rack, remove the pan, and cool completely.

cucumber cooler with mint

Serves 4   Preparation **10 minutes**

A cool and refreshing drink that might become your next summer favorite. You can also add raw mango pieces to add a unique flavor to this drink.

3 quarts (3 liters) water, chilled
3 **English cucumbers, peeled and coarsely sliced**
½ **cup (4 g) fresh mint leaves**
½ **cup (125 ml) fresh lime juice**
¼ **teaspoon cumin seeds, toasted and ground (page 7)**
¼ **cup (50 g) sugar**

1 In a blender, add ½ cup (125 ml) of the water and 1 cup (140 g) of sliced cucumber. Blend until smooth. Add more cucumber and mint and blend. Continue until all the cucumbers and mint are puréed.
2 Strain the cucumber juice of its seeds into a very large pitcher. Add the remaining water, lime juice, cumin and sugar. Stir well to combine. Chill before serving.

watermelon cranberry sharbat

Serves 6   Preparation **15 minutes**

This bright red drink is as visually appealing as it is thirst-quenching. A true summertime favorite. Add a good helping of vodka, and this becomes a great idea for a house drink for one of your summer entertainment evenings.

2½ **lbs (1.25 kg) seedless watermelon, rind removed and diced**
1 **cup (250 ml) cranberry juice**
¼ **cup (65 ml) fresh lime juice**
½ **cup (100 g) sugar**
1 **lime, cut into 6 slices**

1 Place the watermelon in a blender or food processor and process until smooth. Pass the purée through a fine-mesh sieve placed over a bowl. Discard the pulp.
2 Pour the juice into a large pitcher. Add the cranberry juice, lime juice and sugar, and stir to combine. Refrigerate until very cold.
3 Pour into tall chilled glasses and garnish with the lime slices.

valrhona chocolate burfi with toasted coconut

Makes **36 pieces**   Preparation **10 minutes**   Cooking **15 minutes**

Burfi is a common Indian confection that is generally made with condensed milk and sugar. Here is my version prepared with my favorite chocolate. Valrhona is an expensive and exotic bittersweet chocolate from Belgium; my favorite to use when making chocolate sweets. It is definitely worth trying out when making desserts and it's easy to find in gourmet stores. However, any popular brand of bitter-sweet chocolate available in your supermarket can be used to make this dish. I have used toasted coconut to lend an Indian twist. You can use hazelnut shavings, or a mixture of crushed dried fruits and nuts, raisins, cashews and almonds for this recipe.

1 cup (200 g) sugar
½ cup (125 ml) water
1 lb (500 g) almond paste, broken up into small pieces
1 cup (210 g) clarified butter
1 cup (200 g) Valrhona chocolate, melted
¼ cup (25 g) almonds, ground
½ cup (50 g) grated sweetened coconut, toasted (page 7)
1 tablespoon confectioners' sugar

1 Combine the sugar and water in a heavy-bottomed medium saucepan and boil together until a candy thermometer registers 225°F (105°C) and a small amount of the syrup forms a thin thread when pressed between the thumb and forefinger.

2 Reduce the heat to medium and stir in the almond paste with ¼ cup (52 g) of the clarified butter. Stir in the rest of the clarified butter slowly until all of it has been absorbed. Keep stirring over medium to medium-low heat. The mixture will become a single mass.

3 Lower the heat and continue stirring until the mixture becomes porous and starts to appear drier, about 10 minutes. Add the melted chocolate and mix to incorporate.

4 Spread the mixture into a 9-in (23-cm) square baking pan and press to compact and even the surface. Immediately sprinkle with the almonds and coconut, gently pressing them into the surface. While still warm, cut into small square or diamond shapes. Dust with sugar and serve at room temperature. This can be stored covered at room temperature for up to a week.

cardamom brownies

Makes **20 brownies**   Preparation **10 minutes**   Cooking **25 minutes**

*Everyone loves a chocolate brownie! Add a twist to this favorite
by adding spices or even chili peppers for a unique taste. I have
added freshly ground cardamom powder, but feel to experiment
with spice packets you would find at your local Indian store, or
in the spice aisle of your supermarket.*

5 oz (140 g) **bittersweet chocolate,
  finely chopped**
1 cup plus 2 tablespoons (2¼
  **sticks/250 g) unsalted butter, at
  room temperature, plus extra for
  buttering pan**
4 **large eggs**
1¼ cups (250 g) **sugar**
**Seeds from 15 cardamom pods,
  ground**
1 cup (135 g) **all-purpose flour, plus
  extra for dusting pan**
1¼ cups (125 g) **pecans, lightly
  toasted and coarsely chopped
  (page 7)**

1 Preheat the oven to 350ºF
(175ºC).
2 Butter a 9 x 12-in (23 x 30.5-cm)
baking pan, fit the bottom with a
piece of parchment paper and dust
the inside of the pan with flour; tap
the excess flour out and set aside.
3 Melt the chocolate in a bowl
over simmering water or with a

microwave oven. Remove the
chocolate from the heat and let it
cool slightly.
4 Beat the butter in a large mixing
bowl with a flexible rubber spatula
until smooth and creamy. Stir in
the chocolate. Gradually add the
eggs one at a time. Whisk and then
add the sugar and ground
cardamom, followed by the flour
and pecans, stirring using a whisk
until all the ingredients are
incorporated. Do not beat or
aerate.
5 Scrape the batter into the baking
pan and smooth the top with a
spatula. Bake for 20 to 25 minutes.
The top of the brownies will be dry,
but a knife inserted in the center
will come out wet with batter on it.
Transfer the pan to a cooling rack
and allow the brownies to cool for
30 minutes.
6 Run a knife around the edges of
the pan and unmold the brownies.
Remove the baking paper, cut the
brownies, and serve.

mango yogurt lassi with saffron

Serves 4 **Preparation 10 minutes**

Lassi is an ever-popular Indian drink. Here I have used vanilla-flavored yogurt and fresh mangoes. You can also use canned mangoes in this drink.

4 cups (975 g) vanilla yogurt
2 ripe mangoes (about 900 g), peeled and cut into chunks or 2 cups (500 ml) canned mango pulp
1 cup (125 g) crushed ice
2 tablespoons sugar
¼ teaspoon saffron strands, toasted and ground (page 7)

Combine the ingredients in a blender and process until the yogurt is frothy. Serve cold.

sparkling ginger-lime cooler

Serves 4 **Preparation 10 minutes**

This cooler was inspired by the ever-popular ginger soda—a favorite childhood drink of mine that I remember fondly from my time in India! This is a variation of that: I've added some sparkling water, mint and pepper, for that extra spike of flavor. You can make a concentrate of this and refrigerate it, and then add the soda or sparkling water as needed before serving.

3-in (7.5-cm) piece peeled and chopped fresh ginger
½ cup (4 g) coarsely-chopped fresh mint leaves
½ cup (125 ml) fresh lime juice
6 cups (1.5 liters) sparkling water or club soda
2 tablespoons sugar
1 teaspoon salt
¼ teaspoon ground black pepper
Several ice cubes

In a blender, blend together all the ingredients, except the ice, until the ginger is puréed. Strain and serve over ice in four glasses.

orange and carrot cooler

Serves **4**   Preparation **10 minutes**

Oranges, apart from being a favorite fruit, are also an essential source of Vitamin C. Although this recipe calls for using fresh carrots, this cooler can also be made by using ready-made carrot juice from the juice aisle in the supermarket.

1 lb (500 g) carrots, peeled and
  diced
1 cup (250 ml) honey
¼ teaspoon fresh ground nutmeg
½ gallon (2 liters) orange juice
10 to 12 ice cubes

In a blender, blend together all the ingredients until smooth. Pass the purée through a fine-mesh sieve placed over a bowl. Serve chilled in a tall glasses over ice.

salted yogurt lassi with cumin

Serves **4**   Preparation **10 minutes**

This is the salted version of the lassi that's popular in India. I have used ground toasted cumin, which not only heightens the taste, but also acts as a digestif after a heavy Indian meal.

4 cups (975 g) whole milk plain
  yogurt
2 cups (500 ml) water
1 cup (125 g) crushed ice
3 teaspoons salt
¼ teaspoon cumin seeds, toasted
  and ground (page 7)
1 tablespoon chopped fresh mint
  leaves
¼ teaspoon cumin seeds, toasted,
  for garnish

In a blender, add the yogurt, water, ice, salt, cumin, and mint. Blend until frothy. Strain and into four glass and serve cold, garnished with the cumin seeds.

index

acknowledgments

I have always been so fortunate to be surrounded with good friends, supporting family and a talented group of professionals, all of whom have made working on this book such a pleasure. The great team at Tuttle Publishing along with Eric Oey and Jon Steever, I thank you for your support. Sambrita Basu, friend and a content consultant on travel and food who always helps me put my thoughts into words. Her blog "Vicarious Journeys" can be found online at sambritabasu.com. The talented photographer Jack Turkel, who makes my vision for the food come alive in the luscious photographs in this book. There are many more people, friends and mentors who I would like to thank, but can't possibly fit on this page. To them I offer big thanks for their continuous support and belief in me. —Hari Nayak (www.harinayak.com)

Published by Tuttle Publishing, an imprint of Periplus Editions (HK) Ltd.

www.tuttlepublishing.com

Copyright © 2012 Hari Nayak

Library of Congress cataloging in process.

ISBN: 978-0-8048-4303-4

16 15 14 13 12
5 4 3 2 1

Printed in Hong Kong   1207 EP

TUTTLE PUBLISHING® is a registered trademark of Tuttle Publishing, a division of Periplus Editions (HK) Ltd.

DISTRIBUTED BY

North America, Latin America & Europe
Tuttle Publishing
364 Innovation Drive
North Clarendon, VT 05759-9436 U.S.A.
Tel: 1 (802) 773-8930
Fax: 1 (802) 773-6993
info@tuttlepublishing.com
www.tuttlepublishing.com

Japan
Tuttle Publishing
Yaekari Building, 3rd Floor
5-4-12 Osaki, Shinagawa-ku
Tokyo 141 0032
Tel: (81) 3 5437-0171
Fax: (81) 3 5437-0755
sales@tuttle.co.jp
www.tuttle.co.jp

Asia Pacific
Berkeley Books Pte. Ltd.
61 Tai Seng Avenue #02-12
Singapore 534167
Tel: (65) 6280-1330
Fax: (65) 6280-6290
inquiries@periplus.com.sg
www.periplus.com

the tuttle story

"books to span the east and west"

Most people are surprised to learn that the world's largest publisher of books on Asia had its humble beginnings in the tiny American state of Vermont. The company's founder, Charles E. Tuttle, belonged to a New  England family steeped in publishing. And his first love was naturally books—especially old and rare editions.

Immediately after WW II, serving in Tokyo under General Douglas MacArthur, Tuttle was tasked with reviving the Japanese publishing industry. He later founded the Charles E. Tuttle Publishing Company, which thrives today as one of the world's leading independent publishers.

Though a westerner, Tuttle was hugely instrumental in bringing a knowledge of Japan and Asia to a world hungry for information about the East. By the time of his death in 1993, Tuttle had published over 6,000 books on Asian culture, history and art—a legacy honored by the Japanese emperor with the "Order of the Sacred Treasure," the highest tribute Japan can bestow upon a non-Japanese.

With a backlist of 1,500 titles, Tuttle Publishing is more active today than at any time in its past—inspired by Charles Tuttle's core mission to publish fine books to span the East and West and provide a greater understanding of each.